Collins Colour Guides

BIRDS
Divers to Owls

COLLINS COLOUR GUIDES

BIRDS
Divers to Owls

CLAUS KÖNIG

Translated from the German by
H. MAYER-GROSS

Illustrated with 150 colour photographs

COLLINS
St James's Place, London

MEANING OF ABBREVIATIONS:

♂ = symbol for male, ♀ = symbol for female; L = length of bird (from bill-tip to tail-tip), Wt. = weight, WS = wingspan. The letters after the scientific names are abbreviations for the names of the authors who first described the birds. Lists of these authors' names and of the meanings of the scientific names of species are to be found in the appendix.

Cover photograph: Puffin
Frontispiece: Coots, also a female Tufted Duck

ISBN 0 00 212039-9

First published in Germany by Chr. Belser Verlag, Stuttgart, under the title EUROPÄISCHE VÖGEL II, in 1967.
Printed in Germany

FOREWORD

The 2nd volume of "European Birds" deals with those European breeding birds which belong to the following orders: divers, grebes, petrels, pelicans and cormorants, storks and herons, flamingos, ducks and geese, raptors, game birds, cranes, waders, doves, cuckoos and owls. Volumes 1 and 2 together present a total of 286 colour photographs – of which the 2nd volume includes 150 – a kaleidoscope of the entire European avifauna. The accompanying text is inevitably a little terser, since 20 more species than in Volume 1 have been illustrated.

To familiarise the reader with the birds of prey which play such a big role in nature, a plate has been included showing the most important species as seen in flight. The details of distribution of individual species outside Europe are necessarily sketchy, due to pressure on space.

A short review introduces the orders of birds to be dealt with. Each kind of bird which is illustrated is described in detail, brief particulars also being given of the remaining species in these groups which breed in Europe. For technical reasons it was impossible to depict all species on the same scale, but precise measurements are contained in the text.

The publishers and I express sincere thanks to all the photographers who have placed prints at our disposal. I am also most grateful to Prof. Dr. E. Schüz and Dr. R. Kuhk for their valuable advice.

Claus König

CONTENTS

Brief review of the Orders in this volume

Divers (Gaviiformes)

The divers are represented by 1 family, Gaviidae, comprising 4 species. They are web-footed, having webs of skin stretching between the 3 forward-pointing toes. The chicks are covered in dusky down and are nidifugous (i.e. they leave the nest soon after hatching).

Grebes (Podicipediformes)

This family comprises 4 genera and 20 species. They are not web-footed, but flattish lobes of skin extend out from each toe. The downy young are mostly light-coloured with dark longitudinal stripes and brightly chequered heads. Nidifugous.

Petrels or Tubenoses (Procellariiformes)

The order comprises 3 families: the albatrosses (Diomedeidae) with 13 species, the petrels and shearwaters (Procellariidae) with 73, and the diving petrels (Pelecanoididae) with 4. Only representatives of the Procellariidae breed in Europe. Their nostrils are elongated in tubular form. Outside the breeding season they live primarily on the open ocean; for breeding they resort to coasts and lay their single egg in crevices under rocks or in walls, in self-dug burrows, or in a few cases on open ledges. The nestlings are covered in down, usually greyish, and stay in the nest-site for 2–3 months before they are ready to fly. Many species are only active over the breeding colonies at night because, it is believed, of their vulnerability to predators such as large gulls.

Pelicans, Cormorants, etc. (Pelecaniformes)

There are 5 families: tropic birds (Phaëthonidae) with 3 species, frigate birds (Fregatidae) with 5, cormorants (Phalacrocoracidae) with 31, gannets and boobies (Sulidae) with 9, and pelicans (Pelecanidae) with 6. Only species belonging to the Phalacrocoracidae, Sulidae and Pelecanidae breed in Europe. All 4 toes are connected by webs.

The cormorants are colonial nesters. The young are naked when hatched and gradually grow a covering of dark down. When fed they thrust their heads right inside the parents' wide-open bill.

Gannets usually breed in huge colonies. The young become covered with white down and remain in the nest until fully feathered. Pelicans are characterised by an enormous throat-pouch below the lower mandible. They "scoop" their food from the water.

Herons, Storks, etc. (Ciconiiformes)

There are 4 families: herons (Ardeidae) with 59 species, ibises (Threskiornithidae) with 28, storks (Ciconiidae) with 17, and hammerheads (Scopidae) with a single species. Only the first 3 are represented in Europe. In the herons the neck is doubled into an S-bend during flight, drawing the head into the "shoulders". Many species breed colonially. The downy young are light grey or brownish in colour. Food for the young is regurgitated into the nest by the parents.

Among the ibises only the Spoonbill *(Platalea leucorodia)* and the Glossy Ibis *(Plegadis falcinellus)* breed in Europe. The Hermit Ibis *(Geronticus eremita)* also did so until the 16th century. Ibises, like storks, carry their necks stretched out in flight.

Two species of stork breed in Europe, building nests in trees or on buildings. As in almost all members of the order, the young stay in the nest until ready to fly. The downy young are whitish.

Flamingos (Phoenicopteriformes)

The only family, Phoenicopteridae, contains 6 species. These birds are remarkable for their clumsy, down-turned beaks. They breed colonially, making nests of mud. The young are at first fed on a reddish secretion, rich in protein, fat and carbohydrates, which is produced in the upper part of the parents' digestive tract.

Ducks, Geese and Swans (Anseriformes)

Two families make up this order: the true ducks, etc. (Anatidae) with 145 species and the screamers (Anhimidae) with 3, none of which occurs in Europe. These birds are web-footed, the webs joining the 3 forward-pointing toes. Some feed by grazing or dabbling, others by diving.

Nest-material is generally just what happens to be on the site. Some species breed in tree-holes. At hatching the young are downy and have their eyes open. They are nidifugous.

Diurnal Birds of Prey (Falconiformes)

There are 5 families with 271 species in all: the true hawks (Accipitridae) contain 205, the falcons (Falconidae) 58, the new world vultures (Cathartidae) 6, the ospreys (Pandionidae) and secretaries (Sagittaridae) 1 species each. Only members of the Accipitridae, Falconidae and Pandionidae breed in Europe. The young hatch with eyes open and a whitish covering of down. They are fed on scraps of dismembered prey; vultures (Accipitridae, Aegypiinae) form an exception in providing food from the crop. All young birds of prey keep to the nest site until fully able to fly, but often scramble around in the vicinity before this. The role in nature of raptors in regulating and removing sick individuals of their prey species was formerly not appreciated, and because of this many species were exterminated from large areas. Even today one often finds birds with a hooked beak persecuted as "vermin".

Game Birds (Galliformes)

These comprise the following families: megapodes (Megapodiidae) with 10 species, curassows (Cracidae) with 38, pheasants, etc.—including the domestic fowl—(Phasianidae) with 165, guineafowl (Numididae) with 7, grouse (Tetraonidae) with 18, turkeys (Meleagrididae) with 2, and hoatzins (Opisthocomidae) with 1 species. Only some species of Phasianidae and Tetraonidae breed in Europe. These birds are nidifugous.

Cranes, Rails, etc. (Gruiformes)

There are 11 families: seriemas (Cariamidae) with 2 species, trumpeters (Psophiidae) with 3, true cranes (Gruidae) with 14, limpkins (Aramidae) with 1, sunbitterns (Eurypygidae) with 1, finfoots (Heliornithidae) with 3, kagus (Rhynchochetidae) with 1, bustards (Otididae) with 23, rails (Rallidae) with 132, roatelos (Mesoenatidae) with 3, buttonquails or hemipodes (Turnicidae) with 16. Only representatives of the Gruidae, Otididae, Rallidae and Turnicidae breed in Europe.

Cranes nest on the ground. The young have brownish down and leave the nest soon after hatching. In flight cranes keep neck and legs stretched out. Bustards have long, sturdy legs. They too nest on the ground; the downy young, brownish with dark spots, are nidifugous. The ♂♂ take no interest in the brood.

Rails mostly favour swampy habitats. The young usually have blackish down and leave the nest soon after hatching.

Buttonquails are about quail-size, and lack hind toes. They occur in level scrub- or grassland. The ♀♀ are more brightly coloured than the ♂♂. The latter alone incubate and tend the young, which they lead from the nest soon after hatching.

Waders, Gulls and Auks (Charadriiformes)

This group is also known as the Laro-Limicolae and comprises 16 families: jacanas (Jacanidae) with 7 species, seed-snipe (Thinocoridae) with 4, sheathbills (Chionididae) with 2, crab-plovers (Dromadidae) with 1, thick-knees (Burhinidae) with 9, oystercatchers (Haematopodidae) with 6, plovers (Charadriidae) with 63, sandpipers (Scolopacidae) with 77, phalaropes (Phalaropodidae) with 3, avocets (Recurvirostridae) with 7, painted snipe (Rostratulidae) with 2, pratincoles and coursers (Glareolidae) with 15, skuas (Stercorariidae) with 4, gulls and terns (Laridae) with 82, skimmers (Rhynchopidae) with 3, and auks (Alcidae) with 22. Only members of the Burhinidae, Haematopodidae, Charadriidae, Scolopacidae, Phalaropodidae, Recurvirostridae, Glareolidae, Stercorariidae, Laridae and Alcidae are found breeding in Europe.

The young are mostly nidifugous; they are clothed in variegated down. In some species, such as those which nest on steep cliffs or in holes, the young remain in or near the nest until well-grown. In most auk species, the chicks jump down to the sea from the ledges where they were hatched when part-grown but still unable to fly.

Doves, etc. (Columbiformes)

Of the three families in this order, one—comprising the dodo and solitaires (Raphidae)—is extinct. When being fed the young thrust their heads between the parents' mandibles and obtain predigested food from the crop. In the first days they receive so-called "pigeon-milk", a highly nutritious secretion. There are 16 species of sandgrouse (Pteroclididae). They are somewhat partridge-like birds having short, thickly feathered legs and generally elongated central tail feathers, and inhabit steppe or desert areas. Their young are nidifugous. The doves (Columbidae) comprise 289 species, of which 5 nest in Europe. The young are nidicolous, not leaving the nest until able to fly.

Cuckoos (Cuculiformes)

There are 2 families: turacos (Musophagidae) with 19 species and cuckoos (Cuculidae) with 128. Only the latter are represented in Europe. In the reproduction of this group all stages are found from the normal fulfilment of parental duties to highly specialised brood-parasitism. The European members are exclusively brood-parasitic.

Owls (Strigiformes)

There are 2 families: barn owls (Tytonidae) with about 10 and typical owls (Strigidae) with about 130 species. Owls, as nocturnal birds of prey, used to be classified together with the hawks, and the mistaken idea that the two groups are closely related is still widespread. In fact they are systematically closer to nightjars and swifts. In behaviour too they differ greatly from the diurnal raptors, and owl eggs are always white. Owlets have whitish down and are blind when newly hatched. Most species hunt by night. Indigestible prey-remains are regurgitated in the form of pellets which, in contrast to the pellets of hawks, contain tiny intact bones. It is said that owls cannot see by day, but this is quite untrue. Because the structure of their eyes is specially adapted they can utilise very faint light to orientate at night, but they cannot see in total darkness. They have better vision than humans by day but are "long-sighted". They rely much on their highly developed sense of hearing to find prey.

Raptors in Flight

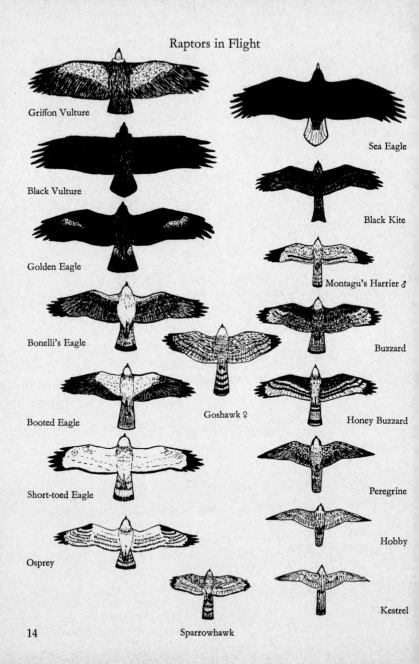

Griffon Vulture

Black Vulture

Golden Eagle

Bonelli's Eagle

Booted Eagle

Short-toed Eagle

Osprey

Goshawk ♀

Sparrowhawk

Sea Eagle

Black Kite

Montagu's Harrier ♂

Buzzard

Honey Buzzard

Peregrine

Hobby

Kestrel

Red-throated Diver · *Gavia stellata* (Pontopp.) Above ▷

Family: Divers (Gaviidae)

Description: In breeding plumage ♂ and ♀ have an ash-grey head, fine white and blackish streaks down the back of the neck, and a sharply demarcated red stripe down the throat. The belly is white, the back dark greyish-brown without distinct speckling. In winter plumage the upperparts are greyer with fine white speckling, the underparts white. Juvenile plumage resembles winter plumage. L: *c.* 23″, Wt: *c.* 4½ lb.

When swimming the head is held erect, and the upward-tilted bill is noticeable. Flying birds use a repeated "kerk" call, and there are weird clanging and wailing notes.

Distribution: Scandinavia and northeast Europe, the Scottish Highlands and islands (also a very few in Ireland), Iceland, Spitzbergen, northern Asia, coastal Greenland, arctic North America. It is a partial migrant in Europe, wintering around coasts and estuaries, more rarely on inland waters; also in the Mediterranean region.

Habitat: Inland waters (often quite small) most often near the sea but at times well inland on mountain lochans, flying to the sea or large waters for feeding.

Breeding: Sexually mature at 2–3 years. The nest—simply a slight hollow, sometimes padded with moss and grass—is very close to water. The eggs, usually two, are elongated and have scattered dark blotches on a brownish ground; both partners share in incubating them for 4–5 weeks. Soon after hatching the young take to the water and are tended by the parents for 2 more months. Single-brooded.

Food: Largely fish, also spawn, frogs, crabs, water insects, worms and snails. The food is almost invariably obtained by diving.

Allied species: The Black-throated Diver (*G. arctica*) differs in summer from the above in having a black throat, fine black and white streaks down the side of the neck, and large white flashes interrupted by fine black lines on each side of the back. In winter it is hard to distinguish from *G. stellata* but its bill is not up-tilted. Its distribution is much as the Red-throated's, but it is absent from Iceland and Ireland; it uses large lochs for breeding, often nesting on islands.

Great Crested Grebe · *Podiceps cristatus* (p. 18) Below ▷

The Great Northern Diver (*G. immer*), larger than most black-throateds, has a black head and chequered black and white back, and breeds in Iceland, various arctic islands, the Greenland coast and northern North America. In winter plumage it is like a heavily built black-throated diver. Both these species winter off British coasts, but the White-billed Diver (*G. adamsii*) usually winters further north. In size and colour it resembles the last species but its bill is yellow-white (not dark) and up-tilted; it breeds in northeast Europe, northernmost Asia and arctic North America.

Great Crested Grebe · *Podiceps cristatus* (L.) (Illustration, p. 16)

Family: Grebes (Podicipedidae)

Description: In breeding plumage ♂ and ♀ have a black crest ending in two tufts, and a rusty neck-frill bordered with blackish-brown. The front of the neck and underparts are white, the upperparts greyish-black. In winter plumage there is a mere hint of the crest, the frill is virtually absent, and the back is grey-brown. Juveniles resemble adults in winter plumage, but have streaked cheeks and sides of the neck. L: 19″, Wt: 2¼ lb.

The most frequent calls, especially when birds are displaying, are a loud "kok-kok", and various trumpeting and rattling noises.

Distribution: Almost all of Europe apart from north Scandinavia and northwest Scotland, large areas of Asia, Africa, Australia, Tasmania and New Zealand. It is partially migratory in Europe, wintering in western, central and Mediterranean regions.

Habitat: Lakes and reservoirs with some aquatic vegetation. Outside the breeding season it may also occur on large rivers, while many move to coasts and estuaries.

Breeding: Sexually mature at 1–2 years. The nest is a floating platform of plant matter attached to reeds, bulrushes, etc. The 3–5 elongated bluish-white eggs acquire a brownish stain during incubation from the decaying nest-material. Incubation is by both sexes, taking close on 4 weeks. The parents look after the young for about 2½ months. 1–2 broods in a year.

Red-necked Grebe · *Podiceps griseigena*

Food: Fish, water-insects, crustaceans, tadpoles, frogs, small snakes on occasion. Virtually all the food is caught by diving.

Red-necked Grebe · *Podiceps griseigena* (Bodd.) (Ill. precedes p. 18)

Family: Grebes (Podicipedidae)
Description: In breeding plumage ♂ and ♀ have the crown black with just a hint of a crest, white cheeks, a red-brown neck and a dark brown back. In winter plumage the cheeks are tinged greyish and the neck is light grey-brown. Juvenile plumage is like the winter plumage. L: 17″, Wt: between 20 and 30 oz.

The calls heard at the time of pair-formation are a kecking, a duck-like quacking and a wailing reminiscent of a horse's neighing.
Distribution: It breeds in Denmark and in a few places in France, Holland and Sweden, becoming steadily more widespread towards the east where it extends from Finland to west Siberia and south to the Balkans and the Caspian Sea; also in east Asia above 45°N and northern North America. In Europe it is a partial migrant, wintering chiefly in the Mediterranean and Black Sea and in lesser numbers in western coastal regions (including eastern Britain).
Habitat: Richly vegetated lakes and pools, less often on open waters; outside the breeding season on inland waters and along seacoasts.
Breeding: It probably first breeds when 2 years old. The nest is generally floating, attached to aquatic plants. The 4–5 whitish eggs acquire brownish discolouration during incubation. This lasts about 22–27 days, both sexes taking part. The young are tended for about 8 weeks after hatching. Single-brooded, sometimes a second.
Food: Fish, water insects and larvae, molluscs, crustaceans, frogs and tadpoles, also some vegetable matter and feathers.
Allied species: In northern Europe, Siberia, the Scottish Highlands, Iceland and northern North America the Slavonian (or Horned) Grebe (*P. auritus*) is found. It is smaller than the foregoing and in breeding plumage characterised by a black flat-crowned head with slender golden ear-tufts and chestnut neck. In winter it has a white neck and cheeks, sharply demarcated from a black crown. It winters mainly around the coast.

Black-necked Grebe · *Podiceps nigricollis* (p. 22) ▷

Black-necked Grebe · *Podiceps nigricollis* C. L. Brehm (Ill. follows p. 19)

Family: Grebes (Podicipedidae)

Description: In summer plumage the head, neck and upperparts of ♂ and ♀ are blackish. There is a fan-like golden yellow ear-tuft behind the eye. The flanks are rusty brown, the belly whitish. In winter dress the back, crown and rear of the neck are dark grey-brown, the cheeks whitish; the dark feathering of the crown extends down below the level of the eyes. The neck is grey-white in front. The up-turned bill of this species affords a good distinction from Slavonian and little grebes in winter plumage. Juvenile plumage is like a pale edition of the winter plumage. L: 12″, Wt: *c.* 10 oz.

The contact note is a squeaking "bribribrib". The trill used in display is composed of multisyllabic phrases.

Distribution: The British Isles (rare), central, southern and eastern Europe, Asia, Africa, North America. It is a partial migrant, wintering in western and southern Europe.

Habitat: Lakes and pools with sizeable extent of open water and lush aquatic vegetation. Outside the breeding season it occurs on biggish lakes and along the coast.

Breeding: Probably sexually mature when 1 year old. The generally floating nest is built of plant matter in the shelter of reeds or rushes. Both sexes build the nest and brood the usually 3–4 eggs, which become brownish during the 3 weeks' incubation. Single-brooded.

Food: Insects and their larvae, especially water-beetles, dragonflies, molluscs, small crustaceans and fish, tadpoles and frogs.

Little Grebe · *Podiceps ruficollis* (Pall.) Above

Family: Grebes (Podicipedidae)

Description: In summer ♂ and ♀ are blackish-brown above, including the area in front of the eyes; the ear-coverts and front of the neck are red-brown. The flanges of the bill are yellowish. In winter plumage the crown and upperparts are dark grey-brown, the cheeks and neck pale brown, and the underparts whitish. Juvenile plumage is like the adult winter. L: 9½″, Wt: 7 oz.

Fulmar · *Fulmarus glacialis* Below

The most striking note is the rippling trill, sounding like "bibibi-bibi...", which may be given in duet during courtship. Besides this, piping and squeaking calls may be noted.

Distribution: The British Isles, southern Scandinavia, central, south and southeast Europe, Asia, North Africa and from south of the Sahara to the Cape. It is resident, apart from the partially migrant east European population which spreads westwards in winter.

Habitat: Lakes, ponds and slow-flowing rivers fringed with water-plants; outside the breeding season on inland waters of all kinds.

Breeding: Breeds when 1 year old. The floating nest is of plant matter among reeds or other aquatic vegetation, but at times quite exposed. The 4–6 whitish eggs, gradually becoming brown, are incubated for 20–21 days by both partners, who then tend the young for 3 further weeks. There are 2, occasionally 3 broods in a year.

Food: As for the black-necked grebe, but more molluscs.

Fulmar · *Fulmarus glacialis* (L.) (Illustration precedes p. 22, below)

Family: Shearwaters (Procellariidae)

Description: The sexes look alike. There are 2 colour-phases: the pale phase has head, neck and underparts white, back and tail light blue-grey, wings grey. In dark-phase birds the white parts are tinged smoky grey. Juvenile plumage resembles the adult's. L: 18½", Wt: between 21 and 30 oz, sometimes heavier.

The effortless gliding flight is a delight to watch. Occasionally a nasal grunting is heard in flight. The birds are very vocal on the breeding ledges, producing loud guttural cackles and crooning noises.

Distribution: Following a dramatic spread it now breeds all round the coast of the British Isles and Iceland; it is also found in west Norway, on islands in the north Atlantic, Arctic, and north Pacific Oceans, the Bering Sea, the Greenland coast and arctic North America. It is a partial migrant, ranging right across the north Atlantic in winter (but some birds are seen on the cliffs again months before the breeding season).

Habitat: Coastal cliffs, stacks and steep banks, sometimes on cliffs a little way inland. Pelagic outside the breeding season.

Cormorant · *Phalacrocorax carbo* (p. 26) Above ▷
Gannet · *Sula bassana* (p. 30) Below ▷

Breeding: It first breeds when 7 or more years old, nesting in colonies. The single pure white egg is laid on a bare ledge, although if soil is present a shallow hollow is formed. Incubation takes about 7–8 weeks. The young fly when some 7 weeks old. Single-brooded.

Food: Small squids, fish and crustaceans, carcases of marine mammals and birds, offal from fishing boats.

Allied species: Leach's Petrel (*Oceanodroma leucorrhoa*), 8″ long, is brownish-grey with pale patches on the inner wing, a white rump with a faint dark line down the centre, and a slightly forked tail. It breeds on a few remote Scottish islands, also islands of the Faeroe group, Iceland, western North America and the north Pacific.

The Storm Petrel (*Hydrobates pelagicus*), 6″ long, is dark greyish with a white rump but without pale wing patches; its tail is square-ended. Nearly all colonies are on islands; they occur in parts of the Mediterranean, Algeria, north Spain, Brittany and the Channel Isles, along the west and north side of the British Isles, the Faeroes and Iceland.

The Manx Shearwater (*Puffinus puffinus*), 14″ long, blackish above and white below, has a very similar distribution. These 3 species winter on the open ocean and many British manx shearwaters reach South America. They are sometimes driven inland by gales (especially Leach's Petrel). All fly close to the water, taking their food on or just below the surface. The breeding colonies (which are sometimes very large) are only approached and left in the dark.

Cory's Shearwater (*Calonectris diomedea*), 18″ long, is grey above, white below and has a yellow bill. It will fly higher above the sea than the other species, and visits its nesting colonies in daylight, except where taken for food by man. It breeds on Mediterranean coasts and islands, and Atlantic islands off Portugal and West Africa.

Cormorant · *Phalacrocorax carbo* (L.) (Illustration follows p. 23, above)

Family: Cormorants (Phalacrocoracidae)

Description: ♂ and ♀ are almost all blackish with a good deal of gloss; there is a sharply demarcated white patch on chin and cheeks. In summer

Shag · *Phalacrocorax aristotelis*

a white patch appears on the thighs, and some have whitish heads. Immatures have whitish underparts. L: 36″, Wt: 5½ lb.

A sonorous "chrochrochro", with manifold variations, may be heard at the nest site, as well as croaking and hissing noises.

Distribution: Eastern Europe, Sardinia, coastal regions of northwest Europe (including the British Isles), the Black and Caspian Seas, parts of Asia Minor and Asia, Australia and New Zealand, west Greenland and northeast Canada. A partial migrant in Europe, its wintering areas are the western and Mediterranean regions.

Habitat: Coasts and estuaries, inland waters with tall trees close at hand.

Breeding: Sexually mature at 3 years. It breeds colonially, nests consisting of sticks, also seaweed, with a lining of finer material. Sites may be on cliffs or rocky islets (as is usual in Britain) or in high trees (often together with herons), sometimes in reedbeds. The 3–5 light blue eggs have a white chalky coating; they hatch after *c.* 4 weeks' incubation by both partners. The young fly after about 7 weeks. Single-brooded.

Food: Predominantly fish, especially eels. They are caught by diving while swimming.

Shag · *Phalacrocorax aristotelis* (L.) (Illustration precedes p. 26)

Family: Cormorants (Phalacrocoracidae)

Description: Both ♂ and ♀ are black with greenish gloss; the bill is slenderer than the Cormorant's, while the gape is yellow. In breeding plumage the head bears a short crest (rather like the wind-blown feathers in the cormorant picture, but further forward). Immatures are more brownish than the adults. L: 30″, Wt: 3¾ lb.

In the breeding season the ♂ has a harsh "arrk-arrk-arrk" call. Hisses, grunts and soft clicking may be heard from the ♀ (and young).

Distribution: Breeds on most suitable seacoasts. Mainly resident.

Habitat: Rocky coasts with steep cliffs.

Breeding: Some reach sexual maturity when 3 years old. A colonial breeder. Nests are of seaweed and any available twigs, etc., on cliff ledges or under boulders on steep slopes. The eggs, most often 3, are like

White Pelican · *Pelecanus onocrotalus* (p. 30) Above ▷
Dalmatian Pelican · *Pelecanus crispus* (p. 31) Below ▷

Cormorants' but smaller. Incubation is mainly by the ♀, taking 30–31 days. Young leave the nest after about 50 days but are still fed for another 3–4 weeks. Single-brooded.

Food: Almost entirely fish. It apparently produces no pellets, presumably digesting bones completely.

Allied species: The Pygmy Cormorant (*P. pygmaeus*) occurs in southeast Europe and southwest Asia. It is the size of a large pigeon and has a brown head and neck.

Gannet · *Sula bassana* (L.) (Illustration follows p. 23, below)

Family: Gannets (Sulidae)

Description: ♂ and ♀ are white with black wing-tips, light yellowish head and neck, and blue-grey bill. Young birds are dark greyish, speckled white; they become whiter over several years. L: 36″, Wt: 6½ lb, WS: *c.* 68″. Deep, barking notes are uttered at the nest site.

Distribution: The world population of the northern form is of the order of 100,000 pairs, and roughly ⅔ of them breed round the British Isles (Scotland has 8 breeding stations, Ireland 2, Wales 1, and England 1—of a few pairs only). Partially migrant, wintering mainly in the North Atlantic. Many juveniles move to tropical Atlantic waters.

Habitat: Cliff-girt coasts, especially islands. Except in the breeding season it stays at sea, but not beyond the Continental shelf.

Breeding: Sexually mature when about 5 years old. Colonies are often large and densely packed, on cliffs (sometimes spreading to level ground above). Nests are of seaweed and grass. The 1 chalky, pale bluish egg is incubated by both partners for *c.* 44 days. After about 75 days the fledgling flies down to the water and then swims out to the open sea, being too heavy with fat to take off again for some days. Single-brooded.

Food: Very largely fish, caught by plunge-diving from various heights.

White Pelican · *Pelecanus onocrotalus* L. (Illustration p. 28, above)

Family: Pelicans (Pelecanidae)

Description: ♂ and ♀ are, apart from black primaries and dark grey secondaries, white tinged with pink. There is a sizeable area of bare,

Heron · *Ardea cinerea* (p. 34)

orange-red skin round the eye. In breeding plumage there is a shaggy crest on the back of the head. Juvenile plumage is predominantly dark brown. L: *c.* 63", Wt: 22–24 lb. ♂♂ are heavier than ♀♀.

The main calls are deep gruntings and croakings.

Distribution: The Danube delta, Black and Caspian Seas, various lakes in Asia, East and South Africa. It winters in the eastern Mediterranean area and Egypt, also southwest Asia and India.

Habitat: Shallows, swampy lakes, large river-deltas; outside the breeding season it occurs on larger inland waters and the coast.

Breeding: Sexually mature at about 3 years. Colonies are usually located in reedbeds, nests being often a mere depression moulded in flood-debris. Both parents incubate the 1–2 white eggs for about 30 days. When the young are partially grown they gather together in flocks. Single-brooded.

Food: Entirely fish, which the birds swim in parties to catch.

Dalmatian Pelican · *Pelecanus crispus* Bruch (Illustration p. 28, below)

Family: Pelicans (Pelecanidae)

Description: ♂ and ♀ are mainly white with a silver-grey sheen; there is a slight curly tuft at the back of the head. Primaries are blackish-brown, secondaries ash-grey. In flight, seen from below, the bird appears whitish except for the wing-tips. The patch of bare skin round the eye is small. Juveniles have head and neck light ash-grey, white undersides, whitish upperparts with scattered dark flecks, dark wings. L: *c.* 66", Wt: 20–29 lb.

Growling, bleating and hissing calls may be heard, also a clappering.

Distribution: The Danube delta (along with the white pelican), the Sea of Azov, the Caspian and Aral Seas, various lakes of southwest and central Asia. Predominantly a resident species.

Habitat: Very similar to the white pelican's, but also mountain lakes.

Breeding: As in the last species, but proper nests of reeds and flood-debris are built. Both partners incubate the usually 2 eggs, which are white and of variable form, for 30–32 days. The young are ready to fly at *c.* 10 weeks. Single-brooded.

Food: Fish, caught by groups of birds swimming along together.

Purple Heron · *Ardea purpurea* (p. 34) ▷

Heron · *Ardea cinerea* L. (Illustration precedes p. 30)

Family: Herons (Ardeidae)
Description: ♂ and ♀ are light bluish-grey above with longish pale grey plumes on the back. The underparts, throat and cheeks are whitish; 2 lines of dark streaks run down the front of the white neck. A black stripe from the eye to the back of the head continues back on each side to form a black crest. The forehead and crown are white, the beak yellow (sometimes flushing red in spring). Juvenile plumage is dingier. L: 36″, Wt: 3¾ lb, WS: 63″.

A harsh "krark" call may be given in flight; at the nest various gurgling and rasping notes are uttered. Nestlings have a chattering begging note.
Distribution: The British Isles, west and south Scandinavia, large areas of Eurasia below 60°N, although only here and there in southwest Europe; also Indonesia and Africa. In Europe the population is partially migrant, wintering in the centre, west and south.
Habitat: Large and small stretches of standing or slow-flowing water, also estuaries, as long as the margins are shallow.
Breeding: Birds first breed when 1–3 years old. Most pairs breed in colonies (heronries). The large nests of sticks are built by both sexes, usually in the crowns of tall trees, at times several to one tree. Colonies on cliffs or among reeds also occur locally. Usually 3–5 matt blue-green eggs are laid. Incubation is shared by the sexes, taking a little under 4 weeks. The young finally leave the heronry, often in small parties, when 8–9 weeks old, but may move from the nest to surrounding treetops when somewhat younger. Usually single-brooded.
Food: Mainly fish, also frogs, mice and voles, moles, lizards, snakes, beetles and other insects, crustaceans, etc.

Purple Heron · *Ardea purpurea* L. (Illustration follows p. 31)

Family: Herons (Ardeidae)
Description: Above, ♂ and ♀ are dark blue-grey tinged with purple, and

Night Heron · *Nycticorax nycticorax* Above in breeding plumage
　　　　　　　　　　　　　　　　　　Below juvenile

have drooping ornamental chestnut plumes. The crown and belly are black, the breast and neck chestnut, with prominent black stripes running down the latter. Young birds are brownish above, paler below. L: *c.* 31″, Wt: 2¼ lb, WS: 55″.

Calls are like those of the heron, but somewhat higher-pitched.

Distribution: The Mediterranean region, middle Europe (local), southeast Europe, southern Asia, Indonesia, Africa, Madagascar. It is mainly a summer visitor to Europe; while a few winter in southern Europe, most do so in steppe regions of Africa south of the Sahara. It is only a rare wanderer to Britain.

Habitat: Swampy areas with large reedbeds, alder and willow thickets.

Breeding: Sexually mature at 1–2 years. It often breeds colonially, nests being placed mainly on flattened reeds, but also in bushes, less often in trees. The usually 4–5 deep blue-green eggs hatch after about 26 days' incubation by both sexes. The chicks can clamber about when 8–10 days old, but always return to the nest. They are ready to fly at 7–8 weeks. Single-brooded.

Food: Much as for the heron. Daily food requirements are *c.* 7–9 oz.

Night Heron · *Nycticorax nycticorax* (L.) (Illustration precedes p. 34)

Family: Herons (Ardeidae)

Description: ♂ and ♀ are black above, with 2 long white crest-feathers drooping from the back of the head. The underparts are white, the wings and tail grey, and the eye ruby-red. Juveniles are grey-brown with heavy whitish flecking above, off-white with darker streaking below; their eyes are light brown. L: 24″, Wt: *c.* 18 oz, WS: 39″.

In flight, especially at dusk, birds utter hoarse "kwack" calls. Quacking and guttural notes are heard at the nest.

Distribution: Southern Europe, sporadic in mid-Europe, east Europe, southwest and south Asia north to Japan, Indonesia, Africa, America. It is a summer visitor to Europe, wintering in Africa south of the Sahara.

Great White Heron · *Casmerodius albus* (p. 38) ▷

Habitat: Marshy areas with bushes, tree-clumps, or scattered trees, thickets in swamps, also extensive reedbeds without trees.

Breeding: It generally breeds at 2 years. Nests are often in colonies, and are built of twigs or reeds, for preference on bushes. The 3–5 blue-green eggs are incubated by both partners for about 3 weeks. The young leave the nest after 3–4 weeks, can fly when 6 weeks old and are independent at 7–8 weeks. Single-brooded.
Food: Frogs, fish, insects, small mammals (mice, etc.), crustaceans, nestling birds.

Great White Heron · *Casmerodius albus* (L.)
(Illustration follows p. 35)

Family: Herons (Ardeidae)
Description: ♂ and ♀ are white and in breeding dress have long delicate plumes lying along the back and extending beyond the tail. There is *no* crest. In summer the bill is black, shading into yellow at the base; it is all black in winter. The legs and feet are blackish. Juvenile plumage resembles the adult winter. L: 35″, Wt: 3½ lb, WS: 63″.

The birds greet each other at the nest with a "grrooo-grrooo". A hoarse croaking may also be heard. Nestlings chatter when food-begging.

Distribution: Southeast Europe, Asia below 50°N, Indonesia, Australia, Africa south of the Sahara, America. It is a partial migrant in Europe, wintering mainly in the Mediterranean region and Africa.
Habitat: Large reedbeds in silted up lakes, river-deltas.

Breeding: Sexually mature at 1–2 years. It nests colonially, often building on flattened reeds; the nest tends to become matted into a solid platform by the end of the season. Incubation of the 4 pale blue eggs takes 25 days, shared by both sexes. The young leave the site when around 6 weeks old. Single-brooded.
Food: Much as for the heron.

Little Egret · *Egretta garzetta* in winter plumage

Allied species: The Squacco Heron (*Ardeola ralloides*), buffish above and white below, with yellow-green black-tipped bill, occurs in southern Spain, France (the Camargue and sporadically north to about Lyons), northern Italy, southeast Europe, southwest Asia and Africa.

The small Cattle Egret (*A. ibis*)—predominantly white but tinged buff on head and back, with a shortish orange-red bill—inhabits Spain and south Portugal, Asia, Australia, Indonesia, Africa, central and northern South America.

Little Egret · *Egretta garzetta* (L.) (Illustration precedes p. 38)

Family: Herons (Ardeidae)
Description: ♂ and ♀ are white, and in summer plumage have long silky plumes on the back, two drooping crest-feathers, and long narrow feathers on the upper breast. The bill and legs are black, the feet yellow. The crest and ornamental plumes are lost after the breeding season. Juveniles resemble winter adults but have no elongated upper breast feathers. L: 22″, Wt: 14 oz, WS: 39″.

The widely audible calls uttered at nest sites comprise croaking, quacking and snarling noises.

Distribution: South and southeast Europe, as far as 45°N in France, Asia, Indonesia, Australia, Africa, Madagascar. This is a summer visitor, spending winter in Africa south of the Sahara and in southern Asia. A few wander to Britain.
Habitat: Swamps with bushes and trees, ricefields, occasionally the sea-coast.

Breeding: It breeds when a year old. Nests are in colonies, made of twigs and similar material, generally on trees and bushes. Incubation of the 3–5 pale blue-green eggs is by ♂ and ♀, and takes about 3 weeks. The young stay in the nest for some 30 days. Single-brooded.
Food: Small fish, frogs, lizards, worms, water-insects.

Little Bittern · *Ixobrychus minutus* (p. 42) Above ♂ ▷
Bittern · *Botaurus stellaris* (p. 42) Below ▷

Little Bittern · *Ixobrychus minutus* (L.)
(Illustration follows p. 39, above)

Family: Herons (Ardeidae)
Description: The ♂ is black above with some greenish gloss, and pale buff on the sides of the head, neck and underparts; it has black wings with light buff coverts. The plumage of ♀ and juveniles is duller, browner and (especially in young birds) heavily streaked. Little bitterns can be recognised in flight by the large pale wing-patches. L: 14″, Wt: 5 oz, WS: 20″.

The display-call of the male is a monotonous "woog woog ..." repeated at regular intervals. Calling is often kept up for long periods, especially on May evenings. An occasional harsh "krer" may be heard from flying birds, while croaking and yapping notes are used at the nest.

Distribution: Eurasia below 60°N, except Iceland, Scandinavia and Britain (where it is a vagrant, perhaps breeding very occasionally). It also breeds in the Middle East, Africa, Madagascar, Australia. European breeders migrate mainly to south and east Africa for the winter.
Habitat: All kinds of inland waters, even small pools, fringed by reeds or swampy vegetation.

Breeding: It is usually sexually mature at 2 years. Many pairs breed alone, but some do so in loose colonies. The ♂ selects the nest site and builds the foundations. The nest is of twigs, reeds and water-plants among broken reeds, sometimes in a bush. Both partners sit on the usually 5–6 eggs, which are pure white without gloss and hatch after 17–19 days. Already at 5–6 days the young can slip from the nest and hide in the reeds if disturbed. When danger is past they return or are called back by the parents. They fly after about 4 weeks. Single-brooded.
Food: Fish, salamanders, frogs and tadpoles, insects, worms and sometimes small nestlings.

Bittern · *Botaurus stellaris* (L.) Left, below; right, cryptic posture blending with reeds.

Family: Herons (Ardeidae)
Description: ♂ and ♀ are, apart from a black crown and whitish throat,

predominantly buffish-brown with darker streaking; the legs are green. Juveniles resemble the adults. L: 30″, Wt: 2¼ lb, WS: 43″.

The best-known note is the booming display-call of the ♂ which is repeated at intervals, particularly in the evening. It consists of a sound like the drawing in of breath, only audible at close quarters, then a powerful "whoomb". From birds flying at night a heron-like "krau" is sometimes heard. Nestlings chatter.

Distribution: Almost all Europe except for the northeast and much of Scandinavia, while it is rare and local in Britain (occurring mainly in the southeast); also northern and southern Africa and large stretches of Asia. The European stock is partially migrant, wintering in the west and around the Mediterranean.

Habitat: Extensive swamps and shallow margins of inland waters with reedbeds; less often smaller pools with a reedbed zone. Outside the breeding season it may also occur by more open ponds, dikes, etc.

Breeding: It mostly begins breeding at 2 years. The ♂ builds several rudimentary nests on laid vegetation among the reeds, one of which is completed by the ♀. ♂♂ are often polygamous. The generally 4–6 matt olive-brown eggs are brooded only by the ♀, hatching after 25–26 days. The ♂ takes no interest in the sitting ♀ or in rearing the young. At 15–16 days the young begin spending some time clambering among the reeds, but return to the nest for the night. After 4–5 weeks they scatter, but they cannot fly properly until 8 weeks old. Single-brooded.

Food: Fish, frogs, newts, reptiles, mice, sometimes young birds; also insects, worms, crustaceans.

Remarks: When danger threatens both the little bittern and bittern adopt a vertical posture with neck stretched upwards which, with the camouflage afforded by streaked plumage, makes them blend perfectly with the surrounding reeds.

White Stork · *Ciconia ciconia* (L.) ▷

Family: Storks (Ciconiidae)
Description: All the contour feathers of ♂ and ♀ are white, as is the tail. The flight-feathers are black, the bill and legs red. In young birds the

legs and bill are black, gradually becoming redder towards the end of the fledging period, but never bright red as in adults. L: 40″, Wt: up to 8 lb, WS: 78″.

Whenever excited, adults begin bill-clappering; this noise is usually prefaced by a hiss. In the greeting ceremony the partners tilt their heads over onto their backs while clappering. Nestlings use mewing calls when begging.

Distribution: It is decreasing in parts of western Europe such as Denmark and Holland and no longer breeds in Sweden or Switzerland. Its strongholds in Europe are in southern Iberia, and from Germany eastwards. It also breeds in North Africa, west and central Asia, a few in South Africa. A summer visitor to Europe, it winters in Africa south of the Sahara down to the Cape. It is a rare wanderer to Britain (supposed to have bred in 1416).
Habitat: Open country with scattered trees or tree-clumps, low-lying or marshy ground; often near habitations.

Breeding: It first breeds at 3–4 years. Nests—frequently on tall buildings, often also in trees—are huge structures of sticks and twigs, lined with finer material. Both partners share in building, and in incubating the 3–5 pure white eggs. These hatch in 32–33 days; the young fly when about 60 days old and become independent some two weeks later. Single-brooded.
Food: Mice, moles, amphibians and reptiles, insects (especially grasshoppers and beetles), worms, also fish and crustaceans.

Black Stork · *Ciconia nigra* (L.) (Illustration follows p. 47)

Family: Storks (Ciconiidae)
Description: The plumage of ♂ and ♀ is predominantly black with purple and greenish sheen; the belly is white. Outside the breeding season the bill and legs are brownish; they become bright red in summer. Juveniles are brown with pale feather-edges above, whitish below, and have light grey-green legs and bill. L: *c.* 38″, Wt: 6½ lb, WS: 78″.

A soft "feeo" is sometimes heard from circling birds; disturbance at the nest elicits a rather loud "hahi", while whistling notes show excitement. Clappering is also reported. Nestlings chatter when begging.

Distribution: Southwest Iberia, a few in Denmark, north and east Germany, eastern Europe roughly south of 60°N, Asia, a few parts of Africa. It is a summer visitor, wintering in Africa.
Habitat: Natural marshy deciduous or mixed woodland, riverside meadows; also areas with no marsh or standing water.

Breeding: First breeds at 3 years. Most nests are in trees, some are on cliff-ledges, exceptionally on the ground. It breeds solitarily as a rule, seldom in loose colonies. The nest, similar to a white stork's, is built by both partners, who also share in the 30-day incubation of the 3–5 white eggs. The young fly at about 62 days, but return to the nest to be fed and to roost for another fortnight. Single-brooded.
Food: Water-insects, fish, frogs, salamanders, also small mammals.

Spoonbill · *Platalea leucorodia* L. (Illustration precedes p. 50)

Family: Spoonbills and ibises (Threskiornithidae)
Description: In breeding dress ♂ and ♀ are white with a yellow-buff gorget and have a crest of faintly yellow-tinged feathers at the back of the head. The long spatulate bill is black with a yellow tip, the legs are black. The crest and gorget are absent in winter plumage. Nestlings and juveniles have pink bills and grey legs. L: 34″, Wt: 4½ lb, WS: *c.* 51″.
   Spoonbills are generally silent. Deep grunts may be heard at the nest, and sometimes a low murmuring when feeding. They can clapper with their bills if excited.

Distribution: South Spain, Holland, southeast Europe, southwest Asia, India, central and east Asia between 30° and 50°N, local in west Africa and the Gulf of Aden. It summers in Europe, and mostly winters south of the Sahara.
Habitat: Swampy areas with reeds or willow and alder scrub, large lakes with shallow vegetated margins, estuarine marshes.

Breeding: It probably only begins breeding at 3–4 years, and is a colonial nester. Both partners build the nest—usually on a flattened patch in a reedbed, in south European Salicornia-steppe often on a bush of this

Black Stork · *Ciconia nigra* ▷

plant, less commonly on a taller bush or tree. The 3–5 white eggs with irregular reddish-brown blotches are incubated by both sexes for about 3 weeks. The young leave the nest after *c.* 4 weeks, and become independent some 4 weeks later. Single-brooded.

Food: Food is mostly gathered in parties, the birds sweeping their bills through the water: fish, water-insects, salamanders, tadpoles, snails and crustaceans.

Allied species: The Glossy Ibis (*Plegadis falcinellus*) breeds in the Guadalquivir delta, northern Italy near Turin, southeast Europe, locally in Asia below 50°N, in Indonesia, Australia, Africa and on islands in the Caribbean Sea. It has a dark brown body with bronzy gloss, blackish-green wings and a sickle-like bill.

Flamingo · *Phoenicopterus ruber* L. (Illustration follows p. 51)

Family: Flamingos (Phoenicopteridae)

Description: In both ♂ and ♀ the whole body is white with a pink flush. They have black flight-feathers, scarlet wing-coverts, pink legs and a pink, dark grey-tipped bill which is down-angled at the centre. Young birds are dingy white with brown wings. L: *c.* 50″, Wt: ♂ *c.* 7 lb, ♀ *c.* 5 lb, WS: *c.* 62″.

The calls comprise goose-like honks and babblings.

Distribution: It breeds in the region of the Guadalquivir delta, the Camargue and the Caspian Sea, also locally in Asia and Africa, Central America, islands in the Caribbean, Guayana. European birds winter in the Mediterranean region.

Habitat: Brackish coastal lagoons with mud-flats or at most sparse marginal vegetation, saline lakes, flat seashores. Other localities are occasionally visited outside the breeding season.

Breeding: Sexual maturity is attained at 5–6 years. The mud nests are grouped in clusters within large colonies; they may be seen in shallow water or on bare mud and look like foot-high tree stumps with de-

Spoonbill · *Platalea leucorodia* (p. 47)

pressions in the centre. ♂ and ♀ build and incubate the clutch, usually 1 whitish egg, for about 30 days. A few days after hatching the young leave the nest and run about in the colony, where they are fed by the parents with a reddish secretion. They start feeding themselves after 40 days and can fly when 10 weeks old. The flamingo is single-brooded, but does not breed at all in years when feeding conditions are unfavourable.

Food: Crustaceans, insect larvae, molluscs, worms, water insects, mud containing tiny organisms, seeds of rushes, etc. The birds stir up small creatures by trampling rapidly with their feet; in feeding the head is held upside down and swept through the water. The bill is adapted for "sieving" food.

Mallard · *Anas platyrhynchos* L. (Illustration follows p. 55)

Family: Ducks, geese and swans (Anatidae)
Description: In breeding plumage the head and upper neck of the ♂ are bottle-green; it has a white neck-ring and red-brown breast. Otherwise it is predominantly shiny grey, with a blue-purple white-edged "speculum" on the wing and black upper and under tail-coverts. Its 4 central tail-feathers are upcurled. The ♀ is largely brown with darker mottling. ♂ and ♀ have orange legs. Juveniles, and the drake in the "eclipse" plumage of late summer, are much like the duck. L: 23″, Wt: 2¼ lb.

The ♂ utters a "rreb-rreb" call, the ♀ gives the familiar "quack-quack-quack".

Distribution: Europe except the extreme north and northeast, large parts of Asia, North America. In Europe it is a resident and partial migrant, birds from the northernmost parts moving south and west.
Habitat: All types of inland waters with aquatic vegetation, even park ponds. Like most duck species, the mallard often occurs in flocks.

Breeding: It breeds when a year old. The nuptial period begins in late autumn with the moult from eclipse to breeding plumage, and lasts until

Flamingo · *Phoenicopterus ruber* ▷

early spring. Pairs are formed at this time. Nests, lined with soft down from the breast of the ♀, are usually fairly near water, occasionally far from it. Most are on the ground, but some ♀♀ lay on pollard willows or in shallow tree-holes, and they take to special baskets hung on trees. The 8–14 pale or buffish green eggs are brooded by the ♀ alone. When leaving the eggs she covers them over with down. Incubation lasts 28 days. The ducklings are led to water by the ♀ as soon as they are dry. If the nest is in a tree they jump to the ground without harm. The young can fly at about 8 weeks. Usually single-brooded; feral and domesticated ducks breed more often.

Food: Predominantly vegetable: both water- and land-plants, seeds, acorns, beechmast, corn; in addition worms, snails, crustaceans, insects and their larvae, tadpoles, small frogs, leeches, sometimes small fish. Mallard often "up-end" while feeding.

Teal · *Anas crecca* L. (Illustration follows p. 59, above)

Family: Ducks, geese and swans (Anatidae)
Description: In breeding dress the ♂ has a dark chestnut head with a curving green strip, narrowly edged white, from the eye to the back of the head. Otherwise it is generally greyish with a horizontal white stripe on the body above the wing. The speculum is green. The ♀, juveniles and the ♂ in eclipse are plain grey-brown with darker mottling. L: 14″, Wt: *c.* 12 oz (the ♀ is usually lighter).

A rather musical "prritt" is often heard from the drake; the ♀ produces a high harsh quacking; both sexes also give "krreck" calls.

Distribution: Europe, except for much of the Mediterranean region; nearly all of Asia above 45°N; North America. European birds are partially migrant, wintering mainly in the west and south.
Habitat: Pools and lakes with rich vegetation, floodwaters, swamps, boggy moorland and woodland pools.

Breeding: General breeding biology is as in the mallard. Nests are concealed in ground-vegetation at varying distances from water. The 7–10 creamy-buff eggs are hatched by the ♀ in 21–23 days. Single-brooded.
Food: Water-plants (duckweed is much favoured), seeds, insects and

their larvae, snails and worms. As with other surface-feeding ducks, the food is largely obtained by "dabbling".

Garganey · *Anas querquedula* L. (Illustration follows p. 59, below)

Family: Ducks, geese and swans (Anatidae)
Description: The ♂ in breeding plumage has a brown head with a broad white band above the eye. Otherwise it is mainly grey-brown with paler sides. White, black-edged scapular feathers droop down from the "shoulders". The front half of the speculum is white, the rear half pale green. The plumages of ♂ in eclipse, juvenile and ♀ are largely grey-brown with darker mottling. L: 15″, Wt: between 9 and 14 oz.

The ♂ has a hard rattling call; both sexes give a nasal "yeg-yeg" when excited.

Distribution: Middle-Europe, sporadic in the Mediterranean area and the north. It breeds sparsely in southern England. Also temperate Asia. It is mainly a summer visitor to Europe, wintering in tropical Africa, rarely in southwest Europe.
Habitat: Lakes and pools with lush vegetation in open country, swamps, floodwater. It does not frequent extensive reedbeds. On passage it occurs on all kinds of inland waters.

Breeding: Details are much as for the teal, but the nest is often further from water. The on average 9–10 creamy-buff eggs hatch after 21–23 days' incubation by the ♀ alone. The young become able to fly after 5–6 weeks. Single-brooded.
Food: Broadly similar to the teal's; animal food is favoured.

Wigeon · *Anas penelope* L. (Illustration precedes p. 62, above)

Family: Ducks, geese and swans (Anatidae)
Description: In full plumage the ♂ has a pale yellow forehead and crown, a pinkish breast, and mainly grey back and sides; the rest of the head

Mallard · *Anas platyrhynchos* (p. 51) ♂ and ♀ ▷

55

and neck are chestnut. The white wing-coverts show particularly in flight, and are retained in eclipse plumage, when ♂♂ otherwise resemble ♀♀. The latter, and juveniles, are mainly grey-brown, in part rust-tinged and with darker mottling. ♂ and ♀ have white bellies. L: 18″, Wt: c. 28 oz.

The ♂ produces a whistling "wheeoo", the ♀ a growling "rrarr".

Distribution: Europe above about 54°N, large areas of Asia. It is a partial migrant in Europe, wintering mainly in the west and the Mediterranean area.

Habitat: Lakes and pools with aquatic vegetation, marshland. In winter many frequent estuaries and flat shores as well as the above habitats.

Breeding: Similar to other surface-feeding ducks. The 7–10 light buff eggs hatch after about 3 weeks' incubation by the ♀. Single-brooded.
Food: Seeds, buds, water-plants (including Zostera or "wigeon-grass" on mudflats), insects, molluscs.

Pintail · *Anas acuta* L. (Illustration precedes p. 62, below)

Family: Ducks, geese and swans (Anatidae)
Description: The ♂ in breeding plumage has a dark brown head and upper neck; the white of the chest and lower neck extends upwards in a strip to the ear region. The tail is long and very slender. Eclipse, juvenile and ♀ plumage are predominantly grey-brown with darker mottling. L: 22″, Wt: c. 2¼ lb, ♀ somewhat lighter.

The ♂ utters a low whistle, the ♀ a growling quacking.

Distribution: In Europe mainly above 50°N, sporadically further south, large stretches of Asia above 50°N but down to 45°N in east Asia, North America from 40° northwards. It is a partial migrant in Europe, wintering particularly in the Mediterranean basin, but many winter around the British Isles too.
Habitat: Moorland pools, lakes with broad zones of emergent vegetation, brackish lagoons. Estuaries and floodwaters are favoured in winter.

Breeding: Similar to previous species. The 8–9 greenish-yellow eggs hatch after about 3 weeks' incubation by the ♀. Single-brooded. Fertile hybrids occur between mallard and pintail.
Food: Much as for the mallard.

Allied species: The small Marbled Duck (*A. angustirostris*), grey-brown flecked with white, with a dark grey zone from eye to back of head, breeds in the Mediterranean area and southwest Asia.

The Gadwall (*A. strepera*) breeds principally in eastern Europe, but also locally in Bavaria, Switzerland, the Rhone valley, Holland, Denmark, the south Baltic coast, the British Isles and Iceland. The ♂ in full plumage is mainly slate-grey with paler grey-brown head and neck, black tail-coverts; the speculum is white.

The Shoveler (*A. clypeata*) has a spatulate bill. In breeding dress the drake has a bottle-green head, white neck and chest, dark chestnut flanks and belly. It breeds in Iceland, the British Isles, much of Europe except the southern- and northern-most parts, large areas of Asia and in North America.

Red-crested Pochard · *Netta rufina* (Pall.)
(Illustration follows p. 63, above)

Family: Ducks, geese and swans (Anatidae)
Description: The ♂ in breeding plumage has a fox-red head and upper neck with the rest of the neck and breast deep black, a grey-brown back, white sides and belly, and a red bill. In eclipse it is largely grey-brown with pale cheeks, although the flanks are noticeably lighter and the bill remains red. The ♀ and juveniles are brownish with pale cheeks; they have dark bills with a red band near the end. L: 22″, Wt: *c.* 2½ lb.

Wheezing, soft quacking and creaking calls are uttered.

Teal · *Anas crecca* (p. 54) ♂ Above ▷

Garganey · *Anas querquedula* (p. 55) ♂ and ♀ Below ▷

Distribution: Southern Europe, especially the western Mediterranean area (which is also the main wintering ground for European birds); local in Holland, Germany, etc.; also considerable areas of Asia. European birds are partially migrant. The species is an uncommon straggler to Britain.

Habitat: Edges of lakes with plentiful submerged plant life, open brackish lagoons.

Breeding: It nests for preference in dense reeds or among sedge tussocks which form a natural roof. The 7–11 stone-coloured eggs are brooded by the ♀ for about 26 days. Sometimes two ♀♀ lay in one nest, occasionally also with ♀♀ of other species. Single-brooded.

Food: Stonewort, pondweed, various other water plants and seeds, occasionally small fish, frogs and invertebrates. This is a diving duck, and often feeds under water but also feeds by up-ending.

Allied species: The ♂ Pochard (*Aythya ferina*) in breeding dress has a red-brown head, black throat and breast, grey back and off-white belly; its pale blue-grey bill with black base and tip rule out confusion with the previous species. The dingier, more brownish-grey ♀ has a bill-pattern like the drake's. It breeds somewhat locally over much of Britain, rarely in Ireland; also in central Europe (local), Scandinavia, east Europe, Asia between 40° and 60°N, sporadically in Crete and North Africa. Many northern birds winter in Britain. Deeper lakes and gravel pits are preferred.

Scaup · *Aythya marila* (L.) (Illustration precedes p. 66, below)

Family: Ducks, geese and swans (Anatidae)

Description: In full plumage the ♂ has a black head with green gloss, a black neck and breast, a light vermiculated grey back, pure white flanks and belly, and yellow eyes. The ♀ is predominantly grey-brown with

Wigeon · *Anas penelope* (p. 55) ♂ Above

Pintail · *Anas acuta* (p. 58) ♂ Below

pale flanks and belly and has a broad, sharply defined white area around the base of the bill. Juveniles resemble the ♀, as does the ♂ in eclipse, although it can still be recognised from the ♀ by its back-pattern. L: 19″, Wt: *c.* 2½ lb.

The main call is a deep "karr".

Distribution: Iceland, the Faeroes, north Scotland (very rare), Scandinavia, northeast Europe, Asia above 65°N, north Canada and Alaska. It is a partial migrant in Europe, wintering around western coasts, also inland in central and southern Europe.

Habitat: Swampy areas, tundra and well-vegetated waters, especially near coasts. Outside the breeding season it resorts to bays and estuaries, and in some regions to fresh-water lakes.

Breeding: Nests are on the ground, often on islands, either among vegetation or quite exposed. The eggs are olive-grey. The breeding biology is generally similar to the tufted duck's.

Food: Larval water-insects and plant matter form part of the summer diet, but the main food comprises mussels and other shellfish, crustaceans, and marine worms, taken by diving.

Tufted Duck · *Aythya fuligula* L.
(Illustration precedes p. 66, above; see also frontispiece)

Family: Ducks, geese and swans (Anatidae)
Description: In full plumage the ♂ is black with sharply demarcated white flanks and belly and a drooping black crest. The ♀ is dark brown, with pale sides and belly and a trace of white at the base of the bill. The adult ♂ never shows this, even in eclipse when it becomes more like the ♀, although not so drab and retaining the tuft. Juveniles resemble the ♀. The species rarely shows much white under the tail. The eyes are yellow. L: 17″, Wt: *c.* 28 oz.

Red-crested Pochard · *Netta rufina* (p. 59) ♂ Above ▷

Goldeneye · *Bucephala clangula* (p. 66) 1 ♂, 2 ♀♀ Below ▷

63

Distribution: Europe (including the British Isles), mainly above 50°N, but locally further south in France, Switzerland, Germany. Also Asia above 45°N. A partial migrant in Europe, it winters in west, central and southern areas and in Africa.

Habitat: Lakes and gravel pits with marginal vegetation, sometimes also ponds in parks, where it becomes quite tame. Outside the breeding season it occurs on all kinds of non-flowing fresh water, very rarely on the sea.

Breeding: The nest is generally close to the water's edge, or even on a mat of floating vegetation. The 8–10 greenish-grey eggs are incubated by the ♀ for 23–26 days. The young become independent and are able to fly at 7–8 weeks. The ♂ participates in guarding the brood. Single-brooded.

Food: Molluscs, worms, less often fish spawn and small fish, also insects and plant matter. It feeds by diving.

Allied species: The Ferruginous Duck (*A. nyroca*) breeds in the Mediterranean region, locally in west and central Europe, but principally in east Europe and large areas of Asia. It rarely wanders to Britain. In full plumage the ♂ is predominantly red-brown with blackish back and white belly and under tail-coverts. In eclipse it resembles the brownish ♀. The eye is white.

Goldeneye · *Bucephala clangula* (L.) (Illustration follows p. 63, below)

Family: Ducks, geese and swans (Anatidae)
Description: In breeding plumage the ♂ has a blackish-green head, a black back, and a white neck and underparts. There is a round white patch between the bill and eye. The ♀ has a mainly grey body, a brown head and white collar above a grey neck. In eclipse the ♂ has a brown

Tufted Duck · *Aythya fuligula* (p. 63) ♂ Above

Scaup · *Aythya marila* (p. 62) ♂ Below

head with indistinct white patch, the ♀ becomes duller. Juveniles resemble the eclipse ♀. In both sexes the shortish bill and sloping forehead give the head a triangular look. The eyes are yellow. L: 18″, Wt: c. 28 oz.

In display the ♂ gives a shrill "kree-eer", at other times a deep nasal "krahkrah". The ♀ produces a hoarse "karr-karr".

Distribution: Chiefly northeast Europe (above 50°N), Scandinavia, the Danube delta, Asia between 50° and 70°N, northern North America. It is a partial migrant in Europe, wintering in the west (including the British Isles), centre and south.

Habitat: Lakes and rivers in wooded areas, marginal vegetation having no importance. Outside the breeding season all kinds of reasonably deep coastal and inland waters.

Breeding: Goldeneyes lay in tree-holes, preferably near water. There is no nest material. The 8–9 blue-green eggs, laid among down plucked from the ♀, are incubated by her for 27–30 days. After hatching the ducklings scramble out of the hole and drop to the ground. They are able to fly after some 8 weeks. Single-brooded. The ♂ takes no part in caring for the brood.

Food: A diving duck, it takes molluscs, insects and their larvae, crustaceans, fish-fry and some plant matter.

Allied species: The similar Barrow's Goldeneye (*B. islandica*) breeds in Iceland, the west coast of Greenland and northwest North America. In breeding dress the ♂ has a row of rectangular white "portholes" along the black back, and a crescentic white patch between bill and eye. The otherwise black head has a purple gloss. In eclipse the two species are very similar.

Long-tailed Duck · *Clangula hyemalis* (L.) Above ▷

Family: Ducks, geese and swans (Anatidae)
Description: The ♂ in summer is mainly brown apart from a white facial patch, white flanks and belly, and has a long, pointed tail. In eclipse in

Smew · *Mergus albellus* (p. 74) 2 ♂♂ Below ♂♂ ▷

late summer it becomes duller and sheds the long tail feathers. These are regrown in the full plumage, acquired in winter when the head, neck, scapulars and flanks are white, the eye-region pale greyish, and the ear-region, breast and centre of back brownish. The ♀ lacks the long tail. She has white sides to head and neck, the crown and ear-region being brown, as is the back. Juveniles resemble the ♀ but show less white. L: ♂ 21″, ♀ 16″, Wt: 18–36 oz.

In winter and spring the ♂ utters a musical, wailing "ah-ah-aaw-wee", and also a nasal, generally disyllabic quacking.

Distribution: Iceland, north Scandinavia, northeast Europe, arctic Asia and North America, the coasts of Greenland and Spitzbergen. It is a partial migrant, wintering largely in the North Sea and Baltic.
Habitat: Lakes and pools in the arctic tundra, at times at quite high altitudes, also fjords; it winters at sea, only odd birds visiting lakes and reservoirs.

Breeding: A few grass and heather stems and much down off the ♀ form the nest, placed among tundra vegetation or in a rocky recess. The 5–8 eggs of varying shades of olive hatch after about 3 weeks' incubation by the ♀. Single-brooded.
Food: Water insects, insect-larvae (especially of gnats), crustaceans, mussels, water-snails, worms, small fish. It feeds by diving.

Allied species: The Harlequin Duck (*Histrionicus histrionicus*) inhabits Iceland, south Greenland, northwest North America and northeast Asia. In breeding plumage the ♂ is largely dark grey-blue with white markings on head, neck and wings, and rusty flanks. The ♀ has a whitish breast; otherwise eclipse ♂, ♀ and juveniles are predominantly dark grey-brown with the face and a small spot behind the eye whitish.

The Velvet Scoter (*Melanitta fusca*) breeds in Scandinavia, northeast Europe, Asia and North America above 50°N; some winter off British coasts. The breeding-plumage ♂ is black with a white spot just behind the eye and a white wing-patch; its bill is mainly yellow. The ♀, juveniles and eclipse ♂ are dark brown with whitish patches before and behind the eye and a white wing-patch.

Eider · *Somateria mollissima* ♂ Above

The Common Scoter (*M. nigra*) is rather like the velvet. However the breeding-plumage ♂ is all black with a mainly orange bill having a black knob at its base; its eclipse plumage is merely duller. ♀ and juvenile are dark brown with pale grey-brown cheeks sharply demarcated from the dark crown. A few breed in north Scotland and Ireland (but many winter around British coasts); the main breeding areas are in Iceland, north Scandinavia, Asia and North America.

Eider · *Somateria mollissima* (L.) (Illustration precedes p. 70, above)

Family: Ducks, geese and swans (Anatidae)
Description: In breeding plumage the ♂ appears largely white with black forehead, crown, flanks, belly and tail; there are green-tinged areas on the nape and side of the head, while the breast is tinged pink. In eclipse the ♂ is black with white on the wings, paler areas above the eye and on the breast. The ♀ is brown, with close darker barring all over. Juveniles resemble the ♀. Immature ♂♂ show peculiar intermediate stages between juvenile and full plumage. L: 23″, Wt: *c.* 4½ lb.

The ♂ utters a crooning "goorooho", while the ♀ produces a grating "kworr" and a deep "gogogog".

Distribution: The coasts of Iceland, northwest Europe (including the northern half of the British Isles), islands of the north Atlantic, the coasts of northeast Asia, North America and Greenland. A partial migrant in Europe, it winters mainly along the northwest seaboard and the Baltic coast.
Habitat: Low-lying rocky coasts, offshore islands being especially favoured, also coastal sand-dunes. Outside the breeding season it is nearly always found on the sea.

Breeding: As a rule Eiders breed in loose colonies. Nests may be close to the shore or some distance inland, among ground vegetation, in clefts among rocks or even on short turf. The clutch of 4–6 olive-green eggs

Goosander · *Mergus merganser* (p. 75) ♂ Above ▷

Shelduck · *Tadorna tadorna* (p. 78) Below ▷

is laid in a thick lining of down, which in places is collected to stuff "eiderdowns". Incubation takes close on 4 weeks. Single-brooded.

Food: This is obtained by diving: mussels and many other kinds of shellfish, crabs, starfish, fish-offal, some seaweed.

Allied species: In Europe the King Eider (*S. spectabilis*) only breeds on the west coast of Norway and in the northeast, possibly also in Iceland. Its range is otherwise similar to the eider's. In breeding plumage the ♂ has an orange facial shield, a pale blue-grey upper head, and a black back. The ♀ is like a duck eider.

The White-headed Duck (*Oxyura leucocephala*) breeds locally in the Mediterranean region, by the Black Sea, in Turkey and southwest Asia. Both sexes are dark brown, the ♂ having a largely white head and bright blue bill, the ♀ pale cheeks crossed by a dark line. The longish tail is often held stiffly upwards.

Smew · *Mergus albellus* L.
(Illustrations follow p. 67, below, and precede p. 70, below)

Family: Ducks, geese and swans (Anatidae)

Description: In full plumage the ♂ is almost completely white with a black line along the rear of the head, black centre of back, and black and white wings. Eclipse, juvenile and ♀ plumage is greyish with whitish underparts, white cheeks and neck and chestnut crown. L: 16″, Wt: *c.* 21 oz.

Occasionally a grating call may be heard. A call like "kwurrick" is given when excited.

Distribution: North Scandinavia, northeast Europe, Siberia; it possibly breeds sporadically further south as well. It is a partial migrant in Europe, wintering mainly in western and Baltic coastal areas, sometimes further south, also not infrequently well inland.

Habitat: Inland lakes and slow-flowing rivers in wooded country. Outside the breeding season it occurs on all types of waters.

Breeding: It nests chiefly in tree-holes, less often in rock-clefts, under scree and in other holes. The nest-hollow is lined with down, which is

Goosander · *Mergus merganser* ♀ Above

also pulled over the eggs if the ♀ leaves. There are usually 7–9 creamy-buff eggs; incubation takes the ♀ about 4 weeks. The young jump to the ground soon after hatching. They are able to fly at about 8 weeks old. Single-brooded.

Food: Small fish, water-insects, crustaceans, molluscs, caught under water.

Goosander · *Mergus merganser* L.
(Illustrations follow p. 71, above, and precede p. 74, above)

Family: Ducks, geese and swans (Anatidae)

Description: In breeding plumage the ♂ has a glossy greenish-black head and blackish back; its breast, underside and flanks are pinkish-white. The ♀ is grey above with chestnut head and white chin. Eclipse ♂ and juvenile plumage resemble that of the ♀. L: (♂) 26″, Wt: *c.* 3 lb, ♀ considerably lighter.

The ♂ utters low quacking notes; those of the ♀ sound like a guttural "karr".

Distribution: Iceland, Scotland and English border counties, the Alps and south Germany, the Danube delta, Scandinavia, northeast Europe, Siberia, locally by the Caspian and in central Asia, North America. European birds are partial migrants, wintering mainly in western coastal regions and the southern Baltic, but also well inland in mid- and south Europe.

Habitat: Lakes, clear rivers and streams with good fish stocks in wooded country, also in treeless areas in the far north, locally estuaries and rocky coastal islets. It frequents mainly inland waters in winter, sometimes also marine bays.

Breeding: It nests chiefly in tree-holes, also hollows among rocks and in banks and walls—usually near water but at times quite far from it. The 7–13 cream-coloured eggs are incubated by the ♀ for 32–35 days. About 2–3 days after hatching the young drop down from the nest-hole. They can fly after about 2 months, but remain with the parents until autumn. Single-brooded.

Food: Fish, crabs, insects, worms, caught under water.

Shelduck · *Tadorna tadorna* (p. 78) ▷

Allied species: The similar but smaller Red-breasted Merganser (*M. serrator*) breeds over much of Scotland and Ireland (recently also in northwest England and north Wales), in Iceland, northern Europe down to Denmark and north Germany, locally in the Crimea, by the Caspian Sea, in Siberia, northern North America, and Greenland. In full plumage the ♂ has a broad band of chestnut around the breast and a "windswept" double crest.

Shelduck · *Tadorna tadorna* (L.) Flight-picture, ♀ on left, ♂ on right.

Family: Ducks, geese and swans (Anatidae)
Description: ♂ and ♀ have a greenish-black head and neck, white body with a chestnut band going right round at "shoulder" level, and a dark stripe down the belly; the flight feathers are black. The bill is bright red, that of the ♂ having a swollen knob at its base in the breeding season. Juveniles are largely grey-brown above, with whitish faces and underparts. L: 24″, Wt: *c.* 2¼ lb.

Calls include a nasal "agagag" and a harsher "ark-ark", as well as a soft "jujuju" used by the ♂ during courtship.

Distribution: Coastal regions of the British Isles and west Europe from north France northwards; also south Spain, the Camargue, Sardinia, Tunisia, Greece, the Black Sea, southwest and central Asia. In late summer most adult Shelducks migrate to certain shallow coastal waters to be safe while moulting their flight-feathers; by far the biggest numbers gather in the Heligoland Bight. They return to their breeding areas in early winter.
Habitat: Flat shores and estuaries where there is mud or sand, sometimes going several miles inland to breed.

Breeding: The nest, a down-lined scrape, is most often in a hole not far from the shore, rabbit burrows being favoured; other sites, e.g. under dense bushes, are sometimes used too. The 7–15 creamy-white eggs hatch after around 4 weeks' incubation by the ♀. The young are soon led to water and are at first tended by both parents; very often several broods join to form a "creche" tended by one of the old birds, the rest of which leave on their moult-migration.

Food: Molluscs, crustaceans, marine worms, fish-fry and spawn, water insects, also some plant matter like algae, grass-tips, etc.

Allied species: The Ruddy Shelduck (*Casarca ferruginea*) is mainly orange-brown with a paler head, the ♂ being characterised by a narrow dark neck-ring. It breeds in south Spain, southeast Europe, north Africa, Turkey and parts of Asia.

Grey Lag Goose · *Anser anser* (L.) Below ▷

Family: Ducks, geese and swans (Anatidae)
Description: Both ♂ and ♀ are predominantly brownish-grey, with pale forewing, and white upper and under tail-coverts. The bill is uniformly orange (western birds) or flesh-coloured; the legs and feet are flesh-coloured. Juveniles resemble the adults. Flocks of this and other species of grey geese fly in V-formation. L: 30–35″, Wt: 6½–7½ lb depending on bodily condition.

The calls are like those of farmyard geese, which are derived from this species. They include cacklings and a nasal "ahng-ank".

Distribution: Iceland, the northern Scottish highlands and Outer Hebrides (also reintroduced elsewhere in Britain), the coasts of Scandinavia, middle-Europe roughly east of the Elbe, southeast Europe and large stretches of Asia. It is a partial migrant: many winter in certain parts of the British Isles and west Europe, other important wintering grounds being in Mediterranean countries.
Habitat: Boggy moorland in the north, marshland and reedy swamps, small islands in lakes and the sea. In winter it feeds on fresh- and salt-marshes and farmland, flighting at dusk to roost on tidal mudflats or on lochs.

Breeding: Birds usually first breed in their 3rd year. The nest is a substantial structure built by the ♀ of any available plant materials, among heather or floating among reeds or in dense vegetation on raised patches in swamps. The 4–8 off-white eggs are laid among down off the ♀; she

Canada Goose · *Branta canadensis* (p. 86) Above ▷

alone incubates them, for about 4 weeks. But the ♂ helps guard the young, which can fly after 8 weeks. Families migrate and remain together in the winter quarters.

Food: Grass-tips, marsh-plants, weeds, clover, seeds, sometimes potatoes.

White-fronted Goose · *Anser albifrons* (Scop.)

Family: Ducks, geese and swans (Anatidae)
Description: ♂ and ♀ are largely grey-brown with black barring on the belly; they have white upper and under tail-coverts. The bill is pink (eastern birds) or orange (Greenland birds); the feet are orange. There is a white shield on the "forehead". Juveniles lack this and the black bars, otherwise they resemble adults. L: 26–30″, Wt: *c.* 5 lb.

The calls are higher-pitched than those of other grey geese and have a "laughing" character, like "kliglig", often rapidly repeated.

Distribution: Northeast Europe, arctic Asia, west Greenland and arctic North America. In Europe the main wintering grounds are in suitable parts of the British Isles, Denmark and the low countries, and parts of southeast Europe. On the Continent migrants often associate with bean geese (*A. fabalis*).
Habitat: Coastal tundra with shallow lakes and swamps. Outside the breeding season it resorts to damp meadows, bogs and saltings.

Breeding: The nest is on the ground among tundra vegetation, thickly lined with down. The generally 4–7 off-white eggs hatch after some 4 weeks' incubation by the ♀. Single-brooded.
Food: Generally as for grey lag goose.

Allied species: The very similar Lesser White-fronted Goose (*A. erythropus*) has a white "shield" extending further over the crown, a yellow eye-ring and a stubbier bill. It breeds in north Scandinavia, northeast Europe and arctic Asia. As European birds normally migrate southeast, very few visit Britain.

Pink-footed Goose · *Anser fabalis brachyrhynchus* Baillon. Above ▷

Family: Ducks, geese and swans (Anatidae)
Description: The pink-footed goose is a subspecies (geographical race) of the Bean Goose (*A. fabalis*). Its head and neck are dark grey-brown; the rest of the plumage is paler, the upper-parts being bluish-grey. The short bill is pink with a black tip and a variable amount of black at the base. The feet are pink. The various races of bean geese are larger and have orange feet and bills, the latter with some black. L: 24–30″, Wt: *c.* 4½ lb.

The nasal calls may be rendered "ung-ung-unk". Those of the bean goose are deeper pitched.

Distribution: East Greenland, Iceland, Spitzbergen. The winter-areas are in localised coastal areas of Great Britain, also nearby parts of the Continent. Bean geese breed in north Scandinavia and from northeast Europe to the Bering Sea; they winter on the North Sea coast of the Continent with a few in Britain; also inland and south to the Mediterranean.
Habitat: It breeds colonially near water, either on tundra or along rocky hillsides and gorges. At other times it is found in similar habitats to the grey lag, and like other geese keeps in flocks.

Breeding: The same nests may be used year after year on rock ledges, flat ground or islands in rivers. The ♀ provides a thick downy lining for the 4–5 whitish eggs and incubates them for about 4 weeks. Single-brooded.
Food: Much as for the grey lag goose.

Allied species: The Snow Goose (*A. caerulescens*) breeds in northeast North America, north Greenland and northeast Siberia. The best-known races are white with black flight-feathers, although immatures are greyer; in one form even adults are grey with only the head and neck white. Individuals of this species sometimes stray to Europe, but some of those reported are in fact escapes from captivity.

Barnacle Goose · *Branta leucopsis* (p. 86) Below ▷

Canada Goose · *Branta canadensis* (L.)
(Illustration follows p. 79, above)

Family: Ducks, geese and swans (Anatidae)
Description: The head and neck are black with a white patch from cheek to chin; the back is brown and the breast pale grey-brown. L: *c.* 40″.
   The flight-call is a trumpet-like "ahong".

Distribution: The Canada goose is native to North America and was introduced in various European parks. It now breeds in a feral state in Britain and Scandinavia, and in Upper Bavaria.
Habitat: Lakes and pools, sometimes tree-fringed, with grassland or marshy ground nearby. Outside the breeding season it often visits fields, and, in some areas, estuaries.

Breeding: Details are basically as for other geese; nests are often in colonies.
Food: Grass, marsh-plants, seeds.

Barnacle Goose · *Branta leucopsis* (Bechst.) (Illustration follows p. 83)

Family: Ducks, geese and swans (Anatidae)
Description: ♂ and ♀ have a black crown, neck and breast, the face and cheeks being white. The back is lavender-grey with dark, pale-edged barring, the belly is whitish. Juvenile plumage differs little from the above. L: 23–27″, Wt: *c.* 2½ lb.
   The calls, usually heard in flight, of a flock of these very sociable geese sound like a pack of small dogs. Gabbling conversational notes are used on the ground.

Distribution: The species breeds on the east coast of Greenland, Spitzbergen and Novaya Zemlya. The wintering grounds are in restricted areas of west Scotland, west Ireland and the North Sea coast of the Continent.

Whooper Swan · *Cygnus cygnus*

Habitat: It breeds along marshy cliff-girt arctic valleys or on open tundra. Outside the breeding season it sticks mainly to grassland close to the shore.

Breeding: A colonial breeder. Most sites are on cliff-ledges or rock-spurs, the same ones being used in successive years. The ♀ provides a lining of down, and usually lays 4–5 pale greenish eggs. General breeding details are as for other geese.
Food: Grass, tundra-plants, algae, moss, also seeds.

Allied species: The Brent Goose (*B. bernicla*) has a dark grey-brown back, black head, neck and breast, with a white patch each side of the neck. The pale-bellied race breeds in Spitzbergen, Greenland and arctic Canada, those from the former two areas wintering largely in western Britain and Ireland. Dark-bellied races breed from Kolguev Island, along northern Siberia to western arctic North America. Some of these populations winter on the North Sea and Channel coasts. In winter this species keeps to bays and estuaries, feeding for preference on "wigeon-grass" (Zostera).

Whooper Swan · *Cygnus cygnus* (L.) (Illustration precedes p. 86)

Family: Ducks, geese and swans (Anatidae)
Description: Adults are white with black legs and feet. The bill is yellow with black at the tip. Juveniles are grey, with flesh-coloured, black-tipped bills. L: *c.* 60″, Wt: 16–27 lb.
   The note used on the water or at take-off is a nasal, grunting "ook"; in flight a trumpet-like "ahng-hoo" is heard.

Distribution: Iceland, north Scandinavia, northeast Europe, Siberia, large stretches of Asia. A few used to breed in Scotland. In Europe it is a partial migrant, wintering (chiefly near coasts) in the British Isles and the northwest coasts of the Continent, as well as further south.
Habitat: Shallow lakes, tundra pools, marshes, slow-flowing rivers in both open and wooded country in the north. In winter it occurs in parties or flocks on or by almost any kind of coastal or inland water.

Mute Swan · *Cygnus olor* (p. 90) ▷

Breeding: Sexual maturity is reached at about 3 years. The nest is of any available aquatic plant material; it is raised up in shallow water or on an island, rarely accessible on the bank. The 5–7 yellowish-white eggs are incubated for about 5 weeks by both partners. The grey downy cygnets take to the water soon after they become dry, and remain with the parents as a family until the end of the winter. Single-brooded.

Food: Marsh- and water-plants, grass, seeds; also a few insects, crustaceans, worms, molluscs and small fish.

Allied species: Bewick's Swan (*C. columbianus*) is smaller, shorter-necked and has much less yellow on the bill (none at all in the American race). It breeds in northeast Europe, arctic Asia and North America. The winter areas include western Europe and the British Isles.

Mute Swan · *Cygnus olor* (Gmel.)

Family: Ducks, geese and swans (Anatidae)

Description: The plumage is white; the orange bill has a black tip and edges and a black knob at the base; the legs and feet are dark grey. Juveniles are grey-brown (rarely white) and have flesh-coloured bills, lacking the basal knob. The bill-pattern—black almost only at the base—distinguishes them from young Whooper and Bewick's Swans. L: *c.* 60″, Wt: from 22 to 44 lb.

Mute swans do not call in flight, but they are the only swans whose wing-beats make a musical humming sound. When annoyed, a shrill snort or a hiss may be produced.

Distribution: The British Isles, south Sweden, middle Europe, the Black Sea area, Asia Minor, the Caspian Sea, locally in Asia. Most central and west European birds stem from semi-domesticated stock. The species is partially migrant (most semi-wild birds are resident), wintering in middle Europe and the British Isles.

Habitat: Semi-wild birds breed on almost any kind of water. Wild stock mostly favour inland lakes with shallow reed-fringed margins.

Breeding: The age of first breeding varies between 2 and 5 years. Wild birds mostly breed among reeds; so do some semi-wild ones, but others make exposed nests on banks or islands. The large nest is of reeds and other plant matter. The usually 5–7 pale greenish eggs are brooded by both parents, hatching after 35–38 days. The cygnets remain with them until winter but are driven off at the approach of the next breeding season. Single-brooded.

Food: Water-plants, grass, seeds, some molluscs, worms and spawn.

Egyptian Vulture · *Neophron percnopterus* (L.) ▷

Family: True hawks and vultures (Accipitridae)
Description: Adults are largely whitish except for the black flight feathers; the yellow skin of face and throat is bare of feathers. The longish feathers at the back of the head look "scruffy". Juvenile plumage is mainly dark brown with black flight-feathers. L: *c.* 24″, Wt: *c.* 4½ lb, WS: *c.* 60″.

Occasionally an almost toneless grunt is uttered.

Distribution: South Europe, the Black Sea region, Africa, southwest Asia, India. It is a partial migrant in Europe, wintering in the Mediterranean area.
Habitat: Mountain country with steep cliffs and ravines, from which it often ranges far over the plains, visiting villages and, locally, larger settlements where it goes mainly for rubbish dumps.

Breeding: Full adult plumage is attained at about 6 years, but it can breed earlier. A cleft or cave in a cliff usually provides the nest-site. Here the 1–2 eggs, whitish with red-brown markings, may be laid on the bare floor. In other cases, bones, rags etc. are brought as nest-material or empty nests of other large birds are taken over. Both parents incubate, the eggs hatching after about 42 days. At first the parents feed a predigested mush to the young. Later the food is brought whole. Usually only one youngster is successfully reared. Single-brooded.
Food: All kinds of offal, carrion, dung, small vertebrates.

Griffon Vulture · *Gyps fulvus* (Hablizl) (Illustration precedes p. 94)

Family: True hawks and vultures (Accipitridae)
Description: The plumage is mainly sandy-brown with black-brown flight-feathers and tail, and white head, neck and ruff. The ruff is reddish-

brown in young birds. The rather long neck, covered with short downy feathers is drawn in when flying. L: *c.* 40″, Wt: *c.* 16 lb, WS: *c.* 99″. Croaking, hissing and deep grunting notes may be heard, also a plaintive whistling in the breeding season.

Distribution: The Iberian peninsula, possibly still in the "Causses" in south France, Sardinia, Sicily, occasionally in the northern Apennines; southeast Europe, southwest and south central Asia, from Turkey to Egypt, North Africa and southeast Africa. It is predominantly resident, but sometimes wanders widely.

Habitat: Open country, bare mountains, rocky gorges.

Breeding: The nest, on a ledge or in a recess of a steep cliff often consists of only a few sticks and feathers. However large stick-nests are also used; these may be old nests of other raptors. Griffon vultures often breed socially. Incubation of the 1 egg—white, occasionally with a few red-brown spots—takes 48–50 days; it is done mainly by the ♀, fed during this period by the ♂ from its crop. At first the chick gets food in the form of a viscid mess regurgitated by the parents. It leaves the nest after about 3 months and becomes independent at about 4 months. Single-brooded.

Food: Meat and entrails from animal carcasses. A "vulture-feast" begins by the birds ripping the ventral skin open with their powerful beaks and then emptying the abdominal cavity.

Allied species: The Black Vulture (*Aegypius monachus*) is similar in size and form to the griffon but is blackish-brown with a brown ruff. It breeds in the south of the Iberian peninsula, Sardinia, Mallorca, Sicily, Greece, the Black Sea area, also large stretches of Asia.

The Bearded Vulture or Lammergeyer (*Gypaëtus barbatus*) has a creamy-coloured head with a black "mask" from eye to beak and black bristly feathers drooping down on each side of the beak. The body is dark greyish above, rusty below, while the flight-feathers and the long, wedge-shaped tail are blackish. Young birds are predominantly brownish. It inhabits high mountain ranges in Iberia, Sardinia, Corsica, Sicily

Griffon Vulture · *Gyps fulvus* (p. 91)

and southeast Europe, besides parts of Asia and Africa. Its preferred diet consists of bones which, if they are too large to swallow, it smashes by dropping them from a height. It shatters the shells of tortoises in the same way. Small vertebrates are caught in hawk-like manner.

Golden Eagle · *Aquila chrysaëtos* (L.) ▷

Family: True hawks and vultures (Accipitridae)
Description: Adults are predominantly dark brown with a golden tinge on head and nape. The legs are feathered right down to the feet. Immature birds are characterised by a white tail with a broad blackish band at the end and a white patch on each wing. The amount of white diminishes with increasing maturity. L: *c.* 32″, Wt: ♂ *c.* 8 lb, ♀ *c.* 10 lb, WS: 79–91″.

The calls occasionally heard are a rather shrill "hiah" and a hoarse, barking "yegyegyeg…".

Distribution: The Scottish Highlands and Western Isles (recently also 1 pair in northwest England), the Alps, Apennines, mountain ranges in the Iberian peninsula, some Mediterranean islands, southeast Europe, Scandinavia and northeast Europe, large areas of Asia and North America, North Africa. It is predominantly resident.
Habitat: Chiefly mountainous country with crags, down to sea-level in places, also in woods in the north. Human persecution has exterminated it from many parts of middle Europe.

Breeding: Sexual maturity is reached at 5–6 years. The eyrie is of sticks, twigs etc., often adorned with green branches, usually placed on a ledge of a steep cliff, occasionally in a tree. A pair often builds 2–3 eyries, breeding in them alternately. The eggs, usually 1–2, are whitish with a varying amount of brownish blotching; they are incubated very largely by the ♀, for 43–44 days. In broods of 2, the weaker eaglet often succumbs to the stronger one's bullying. Eaglets first fly after around 11 weeks and remain with the parents until late winter. Single-brooded.

Food: Mammals up to the size of a fox and birds up to goose-size, also snakes and lizards. The prey is usually killed by a "surprise attack".

Carrion, including bodies of larger animals such as sheep, is eaten too. Stories of wild eagles attacking humans and the taking of babies belong to the realm of mythology. Even someone climbing to an eyrie is in no danger of being attacked.

Imperial Eagle · *Aquila heliaca* Savigny. Spanish race, below.

Family: True hawks and vultures (Accipitridae)
Description: Adults are dark brown above with yellowish feathering on the crown and nape, and blackish below. The square-cut tail has light and dark cross-bands. The Spanish subspecies (*A. h. adalberti*) has conspicuous whitish "shoulders". Immatures have the whole body sandy-brown, darkening with age; there is also darker streaking on their bodies and they have dark flight-feathers. The legs are feathered down to the feet. L: nearly 32″, Wt: around 7 lb, WS: *c.* 79″.

Both sexes utter a barking "krow-krow-krow…".

Distribution: Southern Iberia and north Africa, southeast Europe, Cyprus, southwest Asia and steppe regions of central Asia. The bird is mainly resident, juveniles wander further afield.
Habitat: Open country with single trees or tree-clumps, open woodland on plains, more seldom on high ground.

Breeding: This is much as in the golden eagle. The massive nest is placed in a tree and is often visible from a long distance. Two whitish eggs form the clutch as a rule. Single-brooded.
Food: Mammals up to the size of hares, smaller birds, sometimes carrion.

Allied species: The Tawny Eagle (*A. rapax*) differs from the next two species in having oval nostrils; it is predominantly brown. It occurs from about the northern edge of the Black Sea deep into central Asia, as well as in Arabia and Africa.

The Lesser Spotted Eagle (*A. pomarina*) breeds in east Europe from Greece to 60°N (extending as far west as Brandenburg), also Asia Minor

Booted Eagle · *Hieruaëtus pennatus* Above

and India. Adults are lightish brown, young birds have some white spots on the wings.

The slightly larger Spotted Eagle (*A. clanga*) is darker, immatures having much white on wings and tail-base. Its breeding range lies in moderate latitudes from about 20°E right through Asia. Both these species have round nostrils.

Booted Eagle · *Hieraaëtus pennatus* (Gmel.)
(Illustration precedes p. 98, above)

Family: True hawks and vultures (Accipitridae)
Description: 2 colour-phases occur: dark-phase birds of all ages are dark brown beneath and grey-brown above, with somewhat paler head and nape. In the more frequent light phase the back is grey-brown with pale feather-edges and whitish flecking on the shoulders. The head and neck are pale sandy-coloured, often with a rusty tinge. The underside is whitish with dark streaks, the tail dark grey-brown without a dark terminal band. Juveniles are similar to the adults. L: *c.* 20″, Wt: *c.* 28 oz, WS: *c.* 47″.

The calls sound like "yeg-yeg-yeg", descending in pitch.

Distribution: The Iberian peninsula, Balearic Isles, southern France, southeast Europe and southwest Asia, locally in central Asia, North Africa. A summer visitor to Europe, it winters in tropical Africa.
Habitat: Deciduous and mixed woodland at low and moderate altitudes. It hunts in open spaces.

Breeding: Sexual maturity is probably reached after 3–4 years. During display the ♂ performs aerobatics over the territory, accompanied by frequent calling. The nest is built of twigs in a tree or sometimes on a cliff-ledge. Both partners take turns brooding the generally 2 white eggs, liberally blotched with light brown, which hatch in about 35 days. The young leave the nest after around 7 weeks. Single-brooded.
Food: Small mammals and birds, occasionally also reptiles and large insects (grasshoppers).

Buzzard · *Buteo buteo* (p. 102) ▷

Allied species: Bonelli's Eagle (*H. fasciatus*) is larger but similar in flight-silhouette; the adult has a broad terminal tail-band, and is more or less dark brown above, whitish with fine blackish streaks below. Juveniles are browner. It breeds in the Mediterranean region, southwest and south Asia, and Africa.

Buzzard · *Buteo buteo* (L.) (Illustration follows p. 99)

Family: True hawks and vultures (Accipitridae)
Description: ♂ and ♀ have brown upperparts, narrow light and dark barring across the tail, and light brown to whitish underparts with darker streaking and barring. Buzzards show much individual variation in colour. Juveniles are like adults but show less barring. The eyes are brownish. L: *c.* 21″, Wt: *c.* 2 lb, WS: *c.* 51″.

The best-known call is a mewing "heeoo", heard principally when soaring. A shrill "yick-yick-yick" denotes alarm.

Distribution: Europe, except for east England, Ireland, Iceland, the Faeroes and north Scandinavia; also a large area of Asia, while there are isolated populations in east and south Africa, Madagascar and the islands off west Africa. North European birds are partial migrants, southern ones largely resident.
Habitat: Open wooded country, cultivated land and moorland with trees or cliffs, from sea-level to mountain areas.

Breeding: The age at first breeding is mostly 2 years. The large nest of sticks and twigs, lined with finer material, is placed in a tree or less often on a cliff or bank; it is often used for several years. There are usually 2–3 whitish eggs, lightly or heavily blotched brownish. Incubation is chiefly by the ♀ and takes *c.* 5 weeks. The young fly at about 6 weeks. Both sexes feed them, but mainly the ♀, while the ♂ supplies the prey. Single-brooded.

Sparrow Hawk · *Accipiter nisus*

Food: Small mammals for preference, e. g. rabbits, voles, moles etc., but also reptiles and amphibians and birds. Carrion is often taken in winter, and dead lambs in spring. Other items include worms, molluscs and beetles. It mostly swoops on prey from an elevated perch on a tree, rock, pole, haystack etc., but also in low hunting flight; it occasionally hovers.

Allied species: The similar Rough-legged Buzzard (*B. lagopus*) has its legs feathered down to the feet; apart from this rough-legged buzzards have the front part of the tail white and usually have dark patches at the "wrists" and on the belly—characters which distinguish them from most *B. buteo* individuals. The species breeds in northern parts of Europe, Asia and North America. It moves south in winter, when small numbers also visit eastern Britain.

The Long-legged Buzzard (*B. rufinus*) is larger and has a cinnamon-coloured, usually unbarred tail. It occurs in North Africa, eastern Mediterranean countries and in Asia.

Sparrow Hawk · *Accipiter nisus* (L.) (Illustration precedes p. 102)

Family: True hawks and vultures (Accipitridae)
Description: The ♂ is blue-grey above, whitish below with rufous barring on the breast and fine streaks of the same colour on the throat. The flanks have a reddish tinge. The ♀ is about 1/3 larger, brownish-grey above, whitish below with grey-brown barring and sparse streaking on the throat and neck. The eyes are bright yellow; there are 4 dark bars across the tail. Juveniles have brown upperparts and whitish underparts with heavy barring. L: ♂ *c.* 11″, ♀ *c.* 15″, Wt: ♂ *c.* 4½ oz, ♀ *c.* 8 oz, WS: ♂ *c.* 24″, ♀ *c.* 29″.

It is rather silent; a harsh "kewkewkew" is uttered in the area of the nest.

Goshawk · *Accipiter gentilis* (p. 106) in juvenile plumage ▷

Distribution: Europe, except for Iceland, the Faeroes and the extreme north and northeast; North Africa and large regions of Asia. It is a partial migrant, wintering from west and mid-Europe to the Mediterranean. British breeders are resident.

Habitat: Woodland at all altitudes, often conifer plantations. It also frequents copses in cultivated land and occasionally large parks. It may venture near habitations when hunting.

Breeding: Birds usually breed when 1 year old. In early spring ♂ and ♀, or ♂ alone, soar in circles and perform slow display flights high above the nest-wood. The nest of twigs is built by both sexes, generally at medium height close to a tree-stem, in a well-shaded situation. The presence of whitish body-feathers round the nest is a sign of occupation, since the ♀ moults during the breeding period. The eggs, mostly 4–6, whitish with red-brown blotches, are incubated by the ♀ for 32–35 days. During this period the ♂ brings food, transferring it to her near the nest. The young stay about 4 weeks in the nest. Single-brooded.

Food: The diet is mostly small birds, caught by surprise during fast, low hunting flights. Insects, mice, bats, etc. are also sometimes taken. The sparrow hawk is considered to play an important role in regulating numbers of small birds, a good reason for protecting it.

Allied species: The similar Levant Sparrow Hawk (*A. badius*) has 6–7 bands across the tail. It breeds in southeast Europe, southern Asia, and in Africa.

Goshawk · *Accipiter gentilis* (L.)

Family: True hawks and vultures (Accipitridae)

Description: Adults are grey-brown to slate-grey above, the long tail having 4 broad, dark bands; their underparts are white with dark barring, their talons are yellow. The eyes are orange in the adult ♂, paler in the ♀. Juveniles are brown above, buffish with dark drop-like streaks below, and have yellow eyes. There is an intermediate 1-year old plumage. L: ♂ c. 20″, ♀ c. 24″; Wt: ♂ c. 25 oz, ♀ c. 2½ lb; WS: 40–47″.

A buzzard-like, but higher-pitched "hiah" is occasionally heard. A metallic "gigigigigi..." is uttered near the nest.

Distribution: Nearly all of Europe except the extreme north and Iceland, while breeding records in Britain are extremely rare. It also breeds in Asia and North America. It is mainly resident.

Habitat: Woodland at all altitudes. Extensive woods with tall trees are preferred. When hunting it also appears over open country as long as tree-clumps are present.

Breeding: Birds often begin breeding when 1 year old, still in immature plumage. In early spring display flights similar to the sparrow hawk's are performed. The bulky nests are of twigs and sticks in the crowns of tall trees; a pair often builds several which are used alternately. The 3–4 greenish-white eggs are usually unmarked. Incubation, very largely by the ♀, takes 36–41 days. The young fly when 5–6 weeks old. Single-brooded.

Food: Mammals up to the size of a hare, birds up to chicken-size. A sudden dash is used to take the prey unawares. In some countries the goshawk has been greatly reduced by man, although, being an important regulator in the scheme of nature, it deserves legal protection (which it receives in Britain).

Kite (Red Kite) · *Milvus milvus* (L.) ▷

Family: True hawks and vultures (Accipitridae)

Description: ♂ and ♀ are predominantly reddish-brown with a chestnut tail, grey-white head and black-brown flight-feathers. The eyes are yellowish. In flight the deeply forked tail, also a large grey-white patch near each wing-tip, are characteristic. Juveniles are similar, although their heads are darker. L: c. 24″, Wt: c. 2¼ lb, WS: c. 60″.

Now and then a wailing "wiah-weeay-weeay-weeay" may be heard.

Distribution: South, central and east Europe, local in south Sweden; in Britain only a tiny resident population survives in mid-Wales. It also

occurs in southwest Asia, North Africa and the Atlantic islands off west Africa. European birds are partially migrant, wintering in the Mediterranean region.

Habitat: Deciduous woodland, open ground with copses, tree-belts by water, in both low and hilly areas. In some places it frequents refuse tips or harbours, more rarely rocky coasts with scrub. It is not tied to the proximity of water. Welsh birds live in wooded hillsides and adjacent moors.

Breeding: Sexual maturity is reached at 2 years. In early spring the birds soar over the future nest-site, calling. The nest of sticks and twigs is usually high in a tree. Sometimes several pairs breed close to each other or near black kites or in a heronry. The 2–3 whitish eggs have brown blotching and dark hair-lines; they are incubated by the ♀ for 30–32 days. The young leave the nest after 50–54 days. Single-brooded.

Food: Small mammals and other vertebrates, fish, insects, molluscs, carrion. It sometimes drives other raptors from their prey.

Black Kite · *Milvus migrans* (Bodd.) juvenile plumage Above

Family: True hawks and vultures (Accipitridae)

Description: Adults are predominantly blackish-brown with grey-white heads. The dark-brown tail is slightly forked. Juveniles have paler droplet-like flecking on the dark plumage, and mainly greyish-buff heads. L: *c.* 22″, Wt: *c.* 2¼ lb, WS: *c.* 59″.

The calls are whinnying, sounding like "hee-wewewewew eerr".

Distribution: South, central and east Europe (absent from Iceland, the British Isles and the west). In Scandinavia it only occurs locally in Sweden. Beyond this it breeds in Asia, Australasia, Africa and Madagascar. It is largely a summer visitor, wintering mostly in tropical Africa.

Habitat: More strongly associated with water: woods and copses by inland waters, up to moderate altitudes. It is often seen around heronries.

White-tailed (Sea) Eagle · *Haliaeëtus albicilla* Below

Breeding: Most breed when 2 years old. The species likes to breed in loose colonies. Aerobatic displays are performed by pairs in spring. The nest is of sticks, often with rags and scraps of paper in the lining, usually placed in a biggish tree but sometimes on a cliff, and for preference right in a heronry or cormorant colony. The 2–3 whitish eggs with sparse brown blotches and streaks are incubated by both partners, hatching in 32–33 days. The fledging period is about 6 weeks. Single-brooded.

Food: Floating bodies of small animals, fish, young water-birds, small mammals up to about the size of rats, insects. It also scavenges for scraps and offal in heronries, harbours and refuse dumps.

Allied species: The kestrel-sized Black-winged Kite (*Elanus caeruleus*) is pale grey above, and has black "shoulders" and white underparts; its tail is slightly forked. It breeds in south Portugal, Africa and southern Asia.

White-tailed (Sea) Eagle · *Haliaeëtus albicilla* (L.)
(Illustration precedes p. 110, below)

Family: True hawks and vultures (Accipitridae)
Description: Adults are mainly dark brown with buffish to cream-coloured head and neck. The short, wedge-shaped tail is white. The lower legs (unfeathered) and talons, and the massive bill are yellow. Juvenile plumage is almost entirely brown with a dark tail. L: *c.* 31″, Wt: ♂ *c.* 8 lb, ♀ *c.* 12 lb, WS: *c.* 95″.

A descending series of calls may be heard, like "klikliklikliklakla"—reminiscent of a herring gull; also a harsh croaking.

Distribution: Corsica and probably Sardinia, southeast Europe, a vast area from north Germany east to the Pacific, Scandinavia, Iceland, southwest Greenland. (Exterminated from Britain early this century.) Partially migrant.

Honey Buzzard · *Pernis apivorus* (p. 114) juvenile ▷

111

Habitat: Large stretches of water in open country and wooded areas, also rocky coasts. It is not found among mountains.

Breeding: The age at first breeding is 5–6 years. The large eyrie of sticks and twigs is usually in a tree in woodland, but may be built on a sea-cliff; it is frequently used for a number of years. The 2 chalky-white eggs are incubated mainly by the ♀ for around 6 weeks. The eaglets leave the nest when roughly 3 months old. Single-brooded.
Food: Large fish, waterfowl, smaller land-mammals and seal pups, often carrion.

Allied species: Pallas's Sea Eagle (*H. leucoryphus*) is similar but has a broad white band across its black tail and a dark beak; it inhabits an area from the south Russian steppes to north India and central China.

Honey Buzzard · *Pernis apivorus* (L.) left, juvenile; right, ♀ on nest

Family: True hawks and vultures (Accipitridae)
Description: The upperparts are brown, the head and neck grey-brown to ash-grey, and the underparts light brown to whitish with "teardrop" spotting. There are two narrow bands across the tail near the body and a broad dark band at the tail-tip. In flight the head appears stretched forward, pigeon-fashion, while the bands on the long tail and wave-like lines along the underwing are also noticeable. The eyes are yellow; between them and the upper mandible the feathers are scaly, not bristly as in other hawks. Juveniles resemble adults but are browner, especially below. L: *c.* 22″, Wt: *c.* 28 oz, WS: *c.* 51″.

A plaintive "plee-er" may be heard from soaring honey buzzards.

Distribution: Europe, except parts of the Mediterranean area, the northeast, north Scandinavia, Iceland and most of the British Isles. (A very few breed in southern England.) In Asia it extends to 88°E. A summer visitor, it winters mainly in tropical Africa.
Habitat: Woods with clearings and meadows or other open country around, occasionally in timbered parkland.

114

Breeding: Both partners take part in frequent aerial displays, the ♂ spiralling upwards and then rocketing down with closed wings to the soaring ♀. This is alternated with brief spells of hovering. The nest is of sticks and twigs, usually high in a tree. The nest-cup is regularly decorated with green sprigs and leaves. The eggs (2 as a rule) are heavily marked with chestnut and dark brown; incubation is chiefly by the ♀ and lasts 33 to 35 days. The young fly after about 6 weeks. Single-brooded.

Food: Larvae of wasps and humble bees from ground-nests dug out by the bird; also other insects, small mammals, sometimes ripe fallen fruit.

Marsh Harrier · *Circus aeruginosus* (L.) ▷

Family: True hawks and vultures (Accipitridae)

Description: The ♂ is mostly brown with a streaked buffish head and nape. Its underparts are paler with dark streaking, while its mid-wing and tail are light grey. The ♀ is darker brown, and has whitish crown, nape, throat and "shoulders", her tail and wings being dark brown. Birds in juvenile plumage are chocolate-coloured with creamy-buff crown, nape and throat. As with all harriers, there is something of an owl-like "facial disc". L: *c.* 20″, Wt: *c.* 21 oz, WS: *c.* 51″.

During display-flights the ♂ gives a shrill "cooee"; other calls are a thin "kli-yeh" and chattering noises.

Distribution: Almost all continental Europe (although local in some parts) except for most of Scandinavia and the northeast. Only a few breed in Britain, usually in the southeast. It also occurs over large areas of Asia and in North Africa. It is a partial migrant, wintering chiefly in the Mediterranean region.

Habitat: Extensive reedbeds in open marshy country or by stretches of water.

Breeding: In display-flight the ♂ performs loops and somersaults. The nest is of reeds, twigs etc., built on collapsed reedstems, or on the

ground among reeds, rushes or rank vegetation. The 3–6 (mostly 4) white, sometimes yellow-stained eggs are brooded by the ♀ alone for 32–36 days. The ♂ provides the ♀ with food during this period. When about 35 days old the young leave the nest and scramble among the reeds; they can fly at about 8 weeks. Single-brooded.

Food: Water-birds, small mammals, frogs, snakes and lizards, sometimes also fish and insects. It hunts by quartering the reeds and pouncing suddenly on its prey—chiefly young coots, other rails and water voles (*Arvicola terrestris*).

Montagu's Harrier · *Circus pygargus* (L.) (Illustrations follow p. 119)

Family: True hawks and vultures (Accipitridae)
Description: The adult ♂ is predominantly grey with a paler grey rump. It has black primaries and a black bar on the grey inner wing. Its breast and belly are whitish with rufous streaks on the flanks. In the ♀ the upperparts are dark brown, the rump being white flecked with brown, the tail brown with dark bands across it; the underparts are light brown with dark streaking. Juvenile plumage is dark brown above with rusty edges to the feathers, reddish-buff and unstreaked below. L: *c.* 17″, Wt: *c.* 10 oz, WS: *c.* 43″.

Calls include "keckeck…" or a hoarse "kickick…", and a drawn-out "piah".

Distribution: England (very local), southwest and mid-Europe, south Scandinavia, east Europe, Asia, north Africa; absent from eastern Mediterranean areas. It is a summer visitor, wintering in tropical and southern Africa. All the harriers are rather rare in mid- and west-Europe.
Habitat: Areas of level open country with marshes or reedbeds, also heathland and young forestry plantations, sometimes cornfields and locally sand-dunes.

Breeding: Sexual maturity is presumably reached at 2 years. Display-flights resemble the marsh harrier's. The nest is of rushes, coarse grasses etc. in a trampled area on the ground, usually among tall vegetation. The 3–6 bluish eggs, occasionally with some brown spots, are incubated

by the ♀ for 28–30 days. The ♂ brings food and passes it to her in the air. The young fly when about 5 weeks old. Single-brooded.
Food: Small mammals and birds, insects, frogs and reptiles.

Allied species: The Hen Harrier (*C. cyaneus*) breeds in the northern half of Britain, Ireland, northern Europe and over most of the European range of Montagu's harrier, also in North and South America. Slightly larger than the last species, the colour is similar but the ♂ lacks reddish on the flanks and the bar on the inner wing. However its rump is white, while that of the ♀ is white and unmarked. Juveniles resemble the ♀. In Britain it haunts moorland and young plantations, and occurs along the coast in winter.

The ♂ Pallid Harrier (*C. macrourus*) is like a very pale hen harrier with a pure white underside. ♀ and young resemble those of the hen harrier. This species is found in east Europe and the Asiatic steppes, occasionally wandering as far as the North Sea coast.

Short-toed Eagle · *Circaëtus gallicus* (Gmel.)
(Illustration follows p. 123, above)

Family: True hawks and vultures (Accipitridae)
Description: The upperparts are grey-brown, the underparts more or less white, sparingly streaked brown. The legs and feet are grey, the eyes yellow. There are 3 dark bands across the tail. Juveniles resemble adults. L: *c.* 26″, Wt: *c.* 4½ lb, WS: *c.* 70″.
While soaring, birds utter plaintive "klee" or "kli-ay", also "yu-ock" calls.

Distribution: South Europe, north to about the Loire estuary or perhaps a little further, southwest Switzerland, east Europe, the central Russian steppes, southwest Asia, north Africa. It is chiefly a summer visitor, for the most part wintering south of the Sahara.

Montagu's Harrier · *Circus pygargus* Above ♂ ▷
Below ♀ ▷

Habitat: Open country with scattered tree-clumps; open woodland and woodland-edge; rocky areas with boulder-scree.

Breeding: Sexual maturity is probably only gained after several years. There is much aerial display with soaring and calling. The nest is of branches, twigs and similar material, built usually in a tree, sometimes in a rock-cleft. Incubation of the single white egg is by both partners and takes 40–45 days. The eaglet is fed by ♂ and ♀ and leaves the nest at 70–75 days. Single-brooded.

Food: Snakes of all species, lizards, especially pearl and emerald lizards, slow-worms, sometimes frogs and small mammals.

Osprey · *Pandion haliaëtus* (L.)

Family: Ospreys (Pandionidae)

Description: The upperparts are blackish-brown, the head being white with a dark stripe through the ear-region and a short whitish crest at the rear. The underparts are white with a brownish breast-band. The eyes are yellow, the beak and talons greyish. Juveniles resemble the adults. L: *c.* 22″, Wt: *c.* 3 lb, WS: *c.* 63″.

The calls, heard especially in the nesting area, sound like "kyikyi-kyikyi...".

Distribution: Coastal regions of southern Iberia, Mediterranean islands, Scandinavia, locally in east Europe and Africa, large areas of Asia, Indonesia, coasts of Australia, North America. In Scotland it was wiped out by man early this century but has been breeding again since 1956. It is a summer visitor to Europe, wintering mainly in tropical Africa.

Habitat: Inland waters of all kinds—in woodland and in open country with tree-clumps, also cliff-lined or (less often) sandy coasts.

Breeding: The age at first breeding is 2–3 years. The ♂ performs display-flights over the breeding area, at the same time calling frequently. The substantial nest of sticks and twigs is placed at the top of a tall tree, or on a rocky islet, or (as frequently in south Europe) on a sea-cliff, and is often used for many years. The eggs—mostly 3, sometimes 2—are white

with red-brown blotches. Incubation is chiefly by the ♀, taking *c*. 35 days. The young fly after 8–9 weeks. Single-brooded.
Food: Fish, caught in the talons by plunging down from a height.

Hobby · *Falco subbuteo* L. (Illustration precedes p. 126)

Family: Falcons (Falconidae)
Description: The upperparts are dark slate-grey; the throat and sides of the neck, apart from dark grey moustachial stripes, are whitish. The underside is white with a brownish tinge and heavy dark streaking. The thighs are rusty red. Juveniles are less distinctly marked, being generally browner. The flight silhouette is very like a large swift. L: *c*. 13″, Wt: ♂ *c*. 7 oz, ♀ *c*. 10 oz, WS: *c*. 32″.

Especially near the nest-site a drawn-out "gewgewgewgew…" may be heard, or a piercing "hicke-hicke-hicke-hicke…" when alarmed.

Distribution: Europe except for the northernmost part, Iceland and most of the British Isles (where it breeds only in southern England); North Africa, large stretches of Asia. It is a summer visitor to Europe and winters in Africa.
Habitat: Heathland with scattered trees and clumps, open woodland, parkland, from low levels to a considerable altitude.

Breeding: It first breeds when 2 years old. Aerobatic displays, accompanied by calling, are performed in early summer. Usually 3 eggs, yellow-white densely stippled with brownish, are laid in an old crow's nest and incubated for 28 days by both partners. At first the ♂ brings prey for the young, transferring it to the ♀ in flight. Later it also feeds the young directly. The young fly when 28–32 days old. Single-brooded.
Food: Small birds and large insects, especially beetles and dragonflies. The prey is caught in flight: hobbies are even able to catch swifts (*Apus apus*).

Short-toed Eagle · *Circaëtus gallicus* (p. 119) Above ▷

Peregrine · *Falco peregrinus* (p. 126) Below ▷

Allied species: Eleonora's Falcon (*F. eleonorae*) is like the hobby but larger without red "trousers", and often uniformly dark brown. It breeds, usually colonially, on Mediterranean islands, nesting very late so that it can feed its young on birds migrating south at the end of summer.

The Merlin (*F. columbarius*) is the smallest European falcon. The ♂ is blue-grey above, the ♀ dark grey-brown; both are buffish below with dark streaking. It breeds in Iceland, the Faeroes, Ireland, west and north Britain, north and northeast Europe and northern Asia.

The ♂ of the little Red-footed Falcon (*F. vespertinus*) is almost entirely dark grey with chestnut under tail-coverts and bright red talons. The ♀ has a rusty-coloured crown, a grey back with dark barring, and rusty-buff underparts. It breeds in southeast Europe—sometimes as far west as south Germany, and the Asiatic steppes.

Peregrine · *Falco peregrinus* Tunst. (Illustration follows p. 123, below)

Family: Falcons (Falconidae)

Description: The upperparts are slate-grey, the head somewhat darker. The throat and sides of the neck are white with a broad dark moustachial stripe on each side. The breast and belly are buffish-white with dark, sometimes wave-like barring. Juveniles are dark brown above and have brown moustaches; they are buffish with heavy brown streaking below. In flight-silhouette it is very like a powerfully-built hobby. L: ♂ *c.* 16″, ♀ *c.* 19″, Wt: ♂ *c.* 21 oz, ♀ *c.* 2 lb, WS: *c.* 40″.

In the nesting-area a shrill chattering "kekkekkek..." is uttered; other notes are an almost jackdaw-like "kyack" and a sharp "kozick".

Distribution: Almost all Eurasia, Indonesia, Australasia, Africa, Greenland, North America and the southern tip of South America. In Britain and many other countries—where numbers were being maintained despite human persecution—a very serious decrease has occurred since the mid-1950s, attributed to gradual poisoning through eating prey

Hobby · *Falco subbuteo* (p. 123) in juvenile plumage

contaminated with agricultural pesticides. In Europe juveniles are partially migrant, wintering in the west and the Mediterranean area. Adults are largely resident.

Habitat: Coastal and inland cliffs, especially on moorland; open woodland in some parts of Europe. It often hunts far from its nest. Estuaries are often visited in winter.

Breeding: Breeding begins when 2 years old. Aerobatic displays with much calling occur in early spring. Ledges or crevices of cliffs usually serve as nest sites, but sometimes old nests of other large birds (on cliffs or in trees) are used, and occasionally ledges on tall buildings. The nest is simply a shallow scrape in which the 3–4 densely reddish-marked eggs are laid. The same site is often used for many years in succession. Incubation is mainly by the ♀ and takes about 30 days. The eyasses leave the nest after 5–6 weeks. The ♂ brings food while the ♀ is sitting, passing it to her near the eyrie. Single-brooded.

Food: Chiefly birds, killed by a sudden swoop from aloft, or after a chase; occasionally small mammals and large insects.

Allied species: Rather like the peregrine, but browner, with a pale crown and very thin moustachial stripes, is the Lanner Falcon (*F. biarmicus*). It breeds in central and eastern Mediterranean regions, possibly also in Spain, as well as being widespread in Africa and Arabia.

The Saker Falcon (*F. cherrug*) is brown above with whitish head and throat. The remaining underparts are also whitish, sometimes with a rusty tinge, and marked with streaks of increasing size towards the rear. It inhabits east Europe and large areas of Asia.

The Gyr Falcon (*F. rusticolus*) is of about buzzard-size and either light grey or white with darker wings and dark streaking on the body. It nests in Iceland ("Iceland Falcon"), north Scandinavia, Greenland ("Greenland Falcon", some specimens of which are almost pure white), arctic Asia and North America.

Kestrel · *Falco tinnunculus* L. ♂ left, ♀ right ▷

Family: Falcons (Falconidae)
Description: The ♂ has a blue-grey crown, nape and tail; the rest of the upperparts are chestnut with black spots. It has black flight-feathers,

127

and is pale buff below with darker streaking. The ♀ is reddish-brown above with darker wave-like barring. There is a series of blackish bands across her tail, which (as in the ♂) has a broad blackish tip. Juveniles resemble the ♀. The kestrel hovers a great deal over fields and rough grassland, swooping down at an angle to catch its prey. L: *c.* 13″, Wt: *c.* 7 oz, WS: *c.* 29″.

In flight it is characterised by rather pointed wings and long tail. A piercing "kikikikikiki" may often be heard; other notes like "zickzick" and "krree-krree..." are also used.

Distribution: Europe, except for the extreme northeast and Iceland, almost all of Asia, Africa and Arabia. It is a partial migrant in Europe, particularly in the north and east, from where birds move to milder areas for the winter. This is the commonest falcon in Europe.
Habitat: Farmland with hedgerow timber, coastal and moorland cliffs, open woodland and woodland-edge, sometimes cities.

Breeding: It breeds when 1 year old. Pairs perform aerial displays and call a great deal in spring. Ledges or niches on cliffs and buildings, holes in trees and old nests of hawks, crows or magpies are all frequently used as nest-sites. The usually 4–6 eggs are white, largely covered with reddish-brown markings. They are simply laid on the floor of the chosen site and hatch after 27–30 days' incubation, predominantly by the ♀. The ♂ provides food, transferring it to the ♀ near the nest. The young fly when around 4 weeks old. Single-brooded.
Food: Voles, mice and other small mammals, less often small birds (which are generally caught on the ground); also lizards, frogs, many insects, worms.

Allied species: The slightly smaller but similar Lesser Kestrel (*F. naumanni*) is distinguished by having white claws. The ♂ is brighter in tone and has no spots on its back; the ♀ is very like a ♀ kestrel. It breeds in colonies, in the Mediterranean area, southeast Europe, North Africa and Asia.

Kestrel · *Falco tinnunculus* (p. 127) ♀

Ptarmigan · *Lagopus mutus* (Montin) Summer plumage ▷

Family: Grouse (Tetraonidae)

Description: The winter plumage is pure white except for black sides to the tail; the ♂ also has a black mark from bill to eye. There is a small wattle of red skin over the eye. In summer plumage the ♂ is grey-brown above with dark mottling and has a grey breast, the remaining underparts and the wings being white; the wattles are larger and brighter. The ♀ has the upperparts, throat and upper breast brown with dark mottling, white belly and wings; her wattles are smaller. In autumn the ♂ is a purer grey above. While changing to and from winter plumage, birds may appear chequered white and grey or brown. Juveniles resemble the adults. L: *c.* 13″, Wt: *c.* 16 oz.

The ♂ accompanies its display-flight with a short sequence of crowing notes. Mechanical-sounding, creaking notes are also uttered.

Distribution: The Alps, Pyrenees, Scottish Highlands, Iceland, north Scandinavia, Spitzbergen, Greenland, arctic Asia, Japan, arctic North America. It is a resident.

Habitat: Mountains above the tree-limit—often near unmelted snow, northern tundra; locally (e.g. Iceland) in birch and willow scrub.

Breeding: Birds become sexually mature at 1 year. They keep in pairs during the breeding season. The ♂ calls vigorously in spring, and energetically maintains and defends a territory. The ♀ makes a shallow scrape among rocks, low bushes or sparse vegetation, often lining it with rootlets and bents. The 6–9 light buffish, brown-spotted eggs are incubated by the ♀ alone for 21–24 days. The family stays together until the autumn. Single-brooded.

Food: Shoots, leaves, seeds and berries of rock-plants and mountain-shrubs, also insects. Occasionally scraps in winter.

Allied species: The Willow Grouse (*L. lagopus*) is distributed similarly to the ptarmigan, although it breeds in northeast Europe and is absent from the Alps, Pyrenees, Iceland and Greenland.

The British race is the Red Grouse, which used to be considered a separate species ("*Lagopus scoticus*"). It is found on heather moorland in Exmoor, Wales, northern England, Scotland and Ireland. The plumage

remains reddish-brown with red eye-wattles all year round, whereas the willow grouse has white wings in summer and is almost all white in winter. (The ♂ then has no black on the face.) Both races are usually found on lower ground than the ptarmigan.

Black Grouse · *Tetrao tetrix* L. ♂♂ at mating time

Family: Grouse (Tetraonidae)

Description: The plumage of the ♂ (blackcock) is black above with a bluish sheen, as is the neck and breast. The wings are blackish-brown with white bars. There are large red eye-wattles. The tail-feathers curve outwards to form a lyre-shaped tail. In display these are spread and the white under tail-coverts raised and rendered conspicuous; in addition the wings are drooped. The ♀ (greyhen) is mainly brown with darker barring, and has a slightly forked tail. Juveniles resemble the ♀, although ♂♂ are darker. L: ♂ *c.* 21″, ♀ *c.* 16″, Wt: ♂ *c.* 3 lb, ♀ *c.* 2 lb.

The cocks produce a cooing "kroo-kroor-kroor…". At intervals they stretch or jump upwards and give a hissing "tchooishsh". Hens utter a nasal "gock-gock".

Distribution: Great Britain (excluding southeast England), Scandinavia, north Germany, the Alps, locally over the rest of mid-Europe, large areas of Asia. It is a resident.

Habitat: Moors and peat-mosses with scattered trees and small woods; on high ground generally near the upper woodland limit but sometimes also at lower levels in open woodland with clearings; conifer plantations. A level open space is needed for a "lek".

Breeding: Sexual maturity is reached at 2 years. Blackcocks display communally in spring at special "leks" where each defends a small area and threatens others. The hens visit these leks, and mating takes place there. The ♂♂ take no part in rearing the brood. The ♀ makes a scrape on the ground, sheltered by vegetation, and may add some leaves and grasses as lining. The 7–10 pale yellowish eggs with fine darker spotting are incubated by her for 24–28 days. The young usually remain with her well into autumn. Single-brooded.

Food: Berries, leaf- and flower-buds, seeds, insects. In winter it takes shoots of the previous summer (e.g. bilberry, birch, alder, hazel, larch, pine), also catkins.

Capercaillie · *Tetrao urogallus* L. left, ♂ at mating time; right above ♀ ▷

Family: Grouse (Tetraonidae)

Description: The ♂ is largely dusky in colour. Its black breast has a greenish gloss. It has bright red eye-wattles and a pale horn-coloured bill. The ♀ is predominantly brown with dark mottling. She has a rufous, more or less unmarked breast, and a rounded tail. Juveniles resemble the parents. L: ♂ *c.* 34″, ♀ *c.* 24″, Wt: ♂ 11 lb, ♀ 5½ lb.

"Song" of ♂: notes sounding like tapping on wood are uttered at first in pairs, then gradually speeded up and climaxed by a cork-popping sound, followed by knife-grinding sounds for 2–3 seconds. After a brief pause the whole sequence begins again. Besides this a retching "ah-ergh" may be heard. Hens make a nasal clucking.

Distribution: The Scottish Highlands (reintroduced following extermination), the Pyrenees and Alps, wooded mountain ranges in central Europe, Scandinavia, east Europe, large areas of Asia. Resident.

Habitat: Extensive open mixed or conifer woodland with mature trees and a plentiful berry-bearing ground flora. For display cocks usually pick mature open woodland with scanty undergrowth.

Breeding: Birds do not come into breeding condition before the age of 2 years. Cocks display communally in spring (mid-April to mid-May) at traditional display-grounds, the same spot often being used for decades. The performance is begun before daybreak on certain trees and is followed when it gets light by ground-display, during which the most aggressive cocks "tread" the hens. Unfortunately the shooting of displaying males is still a sport in parts of Europe. The "sportsmen" do not generally realise that the dominant cocks they kill are those most likely to fertilise the ♀♀, and that they may well cause a display-ground to be deserted altogether. The ♀ makes a scrape among bilberry plants

135

or similar vegetation, often at the foot of a tree, lining it with a few grasses and leaves, and takes 26–29 days to incubate the 6–9 eggs, which are pale buffish, rather lightly spotted with reddish-brown. The young often remain with her until late autumn. Single-brooded.

Food: Berries, insects, sometimes small vertebrates; in winter conifer needles, buds of trees and bushes, leaf-tips of ferns and low shrubs.

Allied species: The partridge-sized Hazel Hen (*Tetrastes bonasia*) inhabits the Alps, locally certain hilly areas of central Europe, Scandinavia, east Europe and large stretches of Asia. It is brown above with light and dark barring and streaking and has a grey tail with a dark band across the end. The throat is black in the ♂, pale in the ♀.

Red-legged Partridge (French Partridge) · *Alectoris rufa* (L.)
Below

Family: Pheasants, partridges etc. (Phasianidae)
Description: ♂ and ♀ are mainly a grey-tinged red-brown above with the throat and cheeks white, bordered by a black band which merges below into a series of black streaks. The flanks are heavily barred, the tail and under tail-coverts reddish brown, the bill and legs red. Juveniles are much less bright, and are hard to tell from common partridges. L: 13½", Wt: *c.* 14 oz.

The display-calls of the ♂ sound like "chook-chookerr-chook-chookerr...". When flushed this species calls "gock-gockock-gock...".

Distribution: England and Wales (except the extreme north and west), having been introduced since 1770; France, north Italy and Iberia, Corsica, the Balearic Is., Madeira, the Canary Is. and Azores (introduced). Resident.
Habitat: Dry, often stony country with scrub, vineyards, also farmland (the chief habitat in Britain), chalky or sandy heaths.

Breeding: The species breeds when 1 year old, and is monogamous. The ♂♂ spend long periods delivering their harsh cluckings from a raised

Capercaillie · *Tetrao urogallus* (p. 135) ♀ Above

mound or fence-post, especially in the morning and evening. The ♀ scrapes a nest-hollow and adds a little lining of grass. The usual clutch contains 10–15 eggs, cream-coloured and sparingly spotted with reddish-brown; one partner incubates, for 23–26 days. Apparently the ♀ often lays 2 clutches, of which she broods one and the ♂ the other. The young stay in rather loose coveys with the parent which hatched them until winter.

Food: Seeds, small leaves, buds, grass-shoots, berries, insects, spiders, probably also small snails.

Allied species: The similar Rock Partridge (*A. graeca*) is greyer above; the black band below its white throat is clean-cut, not merging into streaking on the breast. It is found in the Alps, the Apennines, Sicily, southeast Europe and parts of Asia.

The Barbary Partridge (*A. barbara*) has blue-grey eyestripes, cheeks and throat, bordered by a white-spotted chestnut band. It breeds in southern Spain, Sardinia, North Africa, Madeira and the Canary Is.

Quail · *Coturnix coturnix* (L.) ♂ Above ▷

Family: Pheasants, partridges etc. (Phasianidae)
Description: The upperparts are sandy with dark barring and pale streaking. The underparts are cream-coloured with light and dark streaks on the flanks, and spots on the breast. The throat is pale with brown marks in the ♂, pale in the ♀. Juveniles are like the ♀. L: 7″, Wt: *c.* 3 oz.

The call of the ♂ is a ventriloquial, liquid "bick-bibick" or "wet-my-lips".

Distribution: Europe except for the extreme north, most of Scandinavia and Iceland. Also Asia, Africa, Madagascar, Madeira, the Canary Is. and Azores. It is a summer visitor (numbers reaching Britain vary, but are small in most years); European breeders winter in African savannas south of the Sahara.
Habitat: Extensive rough grassland, damp meadowland, cornfields, low bush scrub in south Europe, alpine meadows.

Partridge · *Perdix perdix* (p. 142) ♀ with young Below ▷

Breeding: Quail breed when 1 year old; ♂♂ are mostly polygamous. The 8–16 (usually about 12) eggs are yellowish with dark brown blotches or spots; they are laid in a sheltered scrape on the ground and incubated for *c.* 17 days by the ♀. The young are tended for about 7 weeks, after which they scatter. Single- or double-brooded.
Food: Grass-tips, green plant matter, seeds, small snails, insects.

Partridge · *Perdix perdix* (L.) (Illustration follows p. 139, below)

Family: Pheasants, partridges etc. (Phasianidae)
Description: The ♂ is greyish-brown with buff streaking above; it has a light chestnut head and throat and a rufous tail; there is a chestnut horseshoe-shaped mark on its whitish lower breast. The ♀ is similar but shows only a trace of the horseshoe, while juveniles lack it altogether. L: *c.* 12″, Wt: *c.* 14 oz.

The grating "gitt-rreck" of the ♂ is heard especially in the evening. When flushed ♂ and ♀ give a harsh "grick-grick…".

Distribution: Europe, except for Iceland, much of Scandinavia, most of Iberia, the Mediterranean islands and Greece; it breeds on the Asiatic steppes and has been introduced in North America. Resident.
Habitat: Chiefly farmland and grass downland; high-level pastures in the Pyrenees.

Breeding: Partridges breed when a year old. Pair-formation occurs towards the end of winter, and pairs are maintained during the breeding season. A depression hidden in vegetation or under a hedge serves as nest-site. The 6–25 olive eggs are brooded by the ♀ alone, for 23–26 days. The young stay with the parents as a covey until early the next year. Single-brooded.
Food: Principally seeds, grass-tips and green leaves; some animal food (insects, spiders, arthropods, small snails and slugs, worms) is also taken, mainly in summer. Insect food is essential for small chicks.

Pheasant · *Phasianus colchicus* ♂ Above

Spotted Crake · *Porzana porzana* (p. 146) Below

Pheasant · *Phasianus colchicus* L. (Illustration precedes p. 142, above)

Family: Pheasants, partridges etc. (Phasianidae)
Description: The ♂ is mainly copper-coloured with crescentic black markings. Its very long tail is rufous with black cross-barring. The head and neck are a glossy purplish-green with bright red wattles around the eyes. Many cocks have a white ring round the neck. There is much colour-variation, due to the intermixing of races. The ♀ is buff with dark mottling and has a shorter tail. Juveniles resemble the ♀. L: ♂ *c.* 32″, ♀ *c.* 24″, Wt: ♂ *c.* 3 lb, ♀ *c.* 2¼ lb.

The "crowing" of the ♂ may be written "gott-gock". Hens make clucking sounds.

Distribution: Widely distributed in Asia, it was introduced to Europe as game in ancient times (later also to North America, Australia and New Zealand). At present it is absent only from north Scandinavia, northeast and southern Europe. It is a resident.
Habitat: Arable farmland and parkland with copses, woodland-edge, damp ground and reedbeds.

Breeding: Pheasants breed at 1 year old. Each cock has special displaying sites which it defends against its neighbours. It generally mates with several hens and takes no interest in the broods. The ♀ makes a scrape on the ground, usually hidden under vegetation, in which she lays 6–19 olive or buff eggs. Incubation takes 23–25 days. The chicks are led by the ♀ for a number of weeks. Like other game birds, they can fly short distances when 2 weeks old and still quite small. Single-brooded.
Food: Green plant matter, seeds, grain, berries, peas, insects, worms, snails, small vertebrates.

Allied species: The quail-like Andalusian Hemipode (*Turnix sylvatica*) has a rufous breast and spotted, not streaked flanks; it belongs to the Button Quail family (Turnicidae). It is found in the south of the Iberian peninsula, Africa, India and southeast Asia.

Little Crake · *Porzana parva* (p. 147) Above ♀ ▷
Below ♂ ▷

Water Rail · *Rallus aquaticus* L.

Family: Rails (Rallidae)
Description: The upperparts are dark brown with black streaking; the sides of the head, throat, neck and breast are slate-grey, the belly buffish. The flanks have conspicuous black and white vertical stripes. The bill is long and reddish. Juveniles are duller and have the neck and breast mottled. L: 11″, Wt: *c*. 4 oz.

Water rails lead a secretive life but their weird assortment of calls gives them away, especially on spring evenings. These comprise grunting, groaning, purring and squeaking noises, especially a "krrrooeee" reminiscent of squealing piglets. The display-call of the ♂ sounds like "gup-gup-gupgepgepgirrrr".

Distribution: Europe, apart from north Scandinavia and the northeast; large parts of Asia; local in Africa. It is a partial migrant, wintering in southern and western Europe.
Habitat: Dense vegetation fringing fresh water; fens and swamps.

Breeding: It breeds when 1 year old. The nest of reed-leaves and other available plants is placed on broken-down reeds, sedge-clumps or actually on the ground, always well hidden. The 5–12 eggs are creamy-white, sparsely spotted with red-brown and grey; ♂ and ♀ incubate for close on 3 weeks. The chicks, covered in black down, soon take to the water. They are fully grown and become independent after 6–7 weeks. Single- or double-brooded.
Food: Insects, small crustaceans, molluscs, small frogs, salamanders, sometimes small fish, bits of water plants and seeds.

Spotted Crake · *Porzana porzana* (L.) (Illustration precedes p. 142, below)

Family: Rails (Rallidae)
Description: ♂ and ♀ are brown, generally tinged olive above, with blackish streaks as well as white streaks and speckles. The throat and breast are greyish, the belly off-white, flanks striped white and under tail-coverts buff. The legs and feet are greenish, the bill green with a dark tip and orange base. Juveniles resemble adults but are more heavily spotted. L: 9″, Wt: *c*. 3½ oz.

On evenings and at night in spring and early summer the monotonous display-calls of the ♂ may be heard, sounding like "quit quit quit ...".

Distribution: Europe, except for the extreme north (rare in the British Isles); southwest and central Asia. The European population winters mainly in the Mediterranean region.
Habitat: Lakes, pools and slow-flowing rivers with extensive densely-vegetated shallows; swamps with thick vegetation.

Breeding: It breeds when 1 year old. The nest is of grasses and sedges in a sedge tussock or on the ground, well-concealed by herbage. The 8–14 olive-buff, dark brown-spotted eggs are incubated by ♂ and ♀ for a period of 18–21 days. The young follow the parents for a number of weeks, being fully grown at about 6 weeks. Single- or double-brooded.
Food: Insects, worms, snails, seeds and green parts of marsh- and water-plants.

Little Crake · *Porzana parva* (Scop.) (Illustrations follow p. 143)

Family: Rails (Rallidae)
Description: The ♂ is brown above with blackish and a few pale streaks; its crown and nape are brown, unmarked. Below it is blue-grey with no barring on the flanks, but pale bars on the under tail-coverts. The legs and bill are green, the latter with a reddish base. The ♀ is similar above, but mainly buff beneath with darker barring towards the rear of the flanks, and a white throat. Juveniles resemble the ♀. L: 7½", Wt: *c.* 1½ oz.
 The display-call of the ♂ is a gradually accelerating "beg-beg-beg-begbegbegbeg". The ♀ is said to call "pup-pup-purrr" (Feindt).

Distribution: Sporadic in mid-Europe, south Scandinavia, the Po valley; the main range is from eastern Europe to parts of Asia; local in North Africa. European breeders winter in the Mediterranean region; some also in Africa.
Habitat: Dense reedbeds and swampy zones by lakes and ponds, especially where there are floating plants.

Moorhen · *Gallinula chloropus* (p. 150) ▷

Breeding: Details are much as for spotted crake. Nests are mostly on flattened reeds with stems of surrounding plants drawn together to conceal them from above. The 6–8 eggs are cream-coloured with reddish-brown spots. Incubation, by ♂ and ♀, takes *c.* 3 weeks. Single- or double-brooded.

Food: Broadly similar to that of the spotted crake.

Allied species: Both sexes of Baillon's Crake (*P. pusilla*) look like the ♂ little crake, but they have strongly barred flanks and all-green bills. It breeds in southern Iberia, locally in west and central Europe and south Scandinavia (but is only a vagrant to Britain); also in Asia, south, east and (very locally) north Africa, Madagascar and Australasia.

The Corncrake or Land-rail (*Crex crex*) has dark-streaked brown upperparts, a white chin, light grey-brown neck and breast, and brown flanks with pale barring. It is like other crakes in form and gait. Its grating "errp-errp" call may be heard by day or night. It breeds locally from the British Isles through Europe (except the extreme north and south) to the Asiatic steppes. It particularly favours not-too-dry meadows and has decreased or vanished in areas where earlier machine-mowing is now practised.

Moorhen · *Gallinula chloropus* (L.) (Illustration follows p. 147)

Family: Rails (Rallidae)

Description: ♂ and ♀ are mainly dingy black with dark brown wings. The under tail-coverts and a streak along the flanks are white. The forehead and most of the bill are red, the bill-tip yellow; the legs are green. Juveniles are dark brown with white under tail-coverts and flank-streak and pale throats. They have grey-green bills and legs. L: 13", Wt: *c.* 9 oz.

The main call is a shrill "krerrk"; when agitated sharp "kick-kick" and "kittick" notes are given. The head is jerked while swimming, and the tail twitched while walking.

Distribution: Europe, except for the extreme northeast, north Scandinavia and Iceland; Asia, Indonesia, Africa, Madagascar, southern North

Crane · *Grus grus* (p. 154)

America and large areas of South America. In Europe it is a partial migrant, wintering in the south and west.

Habitat: Standing or slow-flowing fresh water with vegetated margins, ponds—even in parks, marshes, sometimes off-shore islands. It is agile in clambering among vegetation, is often seen swimming on open water, and often dives when danger threatens.

Breeding: The age at first breeding is 1 year. Many nests are just above the water-surface among twigs or aquatic vegetation; others are placed on the bank, while it is not rare to find one in a small tree, built on the old nest of another bird. The ♂ does most of the building. Incubation of the 6–10 eggs, whitish-buff with red-brown and ashy spots, is by ♂ and ♀, taking 19–22 days. The chicks are covered with black down and have red foreheads and yellow bill-tips; once dry they follow their parents in the water. A second nest is often built in which they are brooded. After about 2 weeks the parents prepare for a fresh clutch and spend less time tending the first brood. The young are fully grown at about 6 weeks. Mostly double-, occasionally treble-brooded.

Food: Water insects, worms, molluscs, small amphibians, birds' eggs, green plant matter, seeds, berries, household scraps.

Allied species: The dark bluish Purple Gallinule (*Porphyrio porphyrio*) breeds in the south of the Iberian peninsula, Sardinia, Sicily, by the Caspian Sea, in Africa, south Asia and Australasia. Its legs, frontal shield and bill are red.

Coot · *Fulica atra* (L.) (Illustration opposite title page)

Family: Rails (Rallidae)
Description: ♂ and ♀ are greyish-black all over with a white bill and frontal shield. Juveniles are dark brownish-grey with whitish cheeks, throat and breast. L: 15″, Wt: 18–32 oz.

Great Bustard · *Otis tarda* (p. 155) Above ▷

Little Bustard · *Otis tetrax* (p. 158) ♀ with young Below ▷

Voice: a ringing "kow", often repeated several times; an explosive "pitz".

Distribution: Europe, except for the northeast and northern Scandinavia; large areas of Asia, Australasia, north Africa, the Azores. It is a partial migrant, birds from east Europe wintering in milder western and southern areas.

Habitat: Fresh water with marginal vegetation, but not small ponds or swift-flowing rivers, up to a fair altitude.

Breeding: Coots breed when 1 year old. Territories are staked out in early spring, at times with much quarrelling. Such fights can also occur during the breeding season. Displaying ♂♂ swim about with puffed out wings and head stretched forward. The nest is mostly of reeds or reedmace, usually floating and attached to aquatic vegetation. The 6–9 eggs are pale stone in colour, peppered with fine dark brown spots; incubation, by ♂ and ♀, takes 21–22 days. The downy young are black with orange down on head and neck and red skin on the head. They take to the water as soon as they are dry and are fed by the parents for about 6 weeks. They are fully grown at about 8 weeks. Often double-brooded.

Food: Chiefly water-plants (for which it dives), also insects, snails, small mussels, worms, frog-spawn, tadpoles, small fish and birds' eggs.

Allied species: The similar Crested Coot (*F. cristata*) has two red knobs above the white frontal shield. It breeds in south Spain and Africa.

Crane · *Grus grus* (L.) (Illustration precedes p. 150)

Family: Cranes (Gruidae)

Description: Largely grey; the chin and front of the neck for about half its length are black, as are the forehead and rear of the head; a patch on the crown is red. The cheeks and sides of the neck are whitish, the long legs and the bill grey. Juveniles resemble adults apart from having light brown heads and necks. L: 45″, Wt: *c.* 12 lb, WS: *c.* 88″.

Loud, trumpet-like "krooh" calls are uttered. During display on the breeding grounds a regular "trumpet-fanfare" may be heard; short

Oystercatcher · *Haematopus ostralegus* (p. 159)

unmusical purring notes are used at the nest. The young trill softly. In flight (flocks travel in Vs) the neck and legs are stretched out straight.

Distribution: From northeast Germany and Scandinavia to Siberia; the Danube delta; the Crimea, southwest Asia. It is a summer visitor, wintering in Africa, especially in the White Nile region.

Habitat: Extensive areas of swamp with some tall vegetation, open marshy woodland, reedbeds in south Europe. Also farmland during migration.

Breeding: Sexual maturity is reached at 5–6 years. The birds mostly arrive paired on the breeding grounds; they mate for life. When displaying, birds run round in circles with spread wings and make bows. Nests are on marshy ground, are difficult to get to, and are made of any available plants. The usually 2 olive-grey, brown-spotted eggs are incubated by ♂ and ♀ for 4 weeks. The chicks slither from the nest quite soon after hatching. At 3 days they can run and follow the parents. They are able to fly at 9–10 weeks, but stay with the parents until autumn. Single-brooded.

Food: Insects and their larvae, small vertebrates, green plant matter and seeds including grain.

Allied species: The Demoiselle Crane (*Anthropoides virgo*) breeds in the Black Sea region, by the Caspian and in Tunisia. It is largely grey but has a black chin, neck and breast, and white, drooping ear-tufts.

Great Bustard · *Otis tarda* L. (Illustration follows p. 151, above)

Family: Bustards (Otididae)

Description: The ♂ is red-brown with black wavy barring above, whitish below; its head and neck are grey, and tufts of white moustachial feathers arise at the base of the bill. The flight-feathers are blackish, the wing-coverts white. The ♀ and juveniles are similar but lack moustachial feathers. In flight the neck is stretched forward; the dark primaries and

Spur-winged Plover · *Vanellus spinosus* (p. 162) Above ▷

Lapwing (Peewit) · *Vanellus vanellus* (p. 163) ▷

large white areas on the wing are conspicuous. L: ♂ *c.* 41″, ♀ smaller;
Wt: ♂ 24–26 lb, ♀ *c.* 9–11 lb.

Voice: usually just a hoarse, snoring bark.

Distribution: The Iberian peninsula, northeast Germany, southeast
Europe, steppes of central Asia, Asia Minor, North Africa. A resident
and partial migrant: some mid-European birds move to the Mediterranean region, many stay in the breeding area.

Habitat: Open, more or less level country with short vegetation, and
steppes; in mid- and southwest Europe also in treeless farmland with
extensive corn or rape fields.

Breeding: Sexual maturity is reached at 4–5 years. Flocks disperse in
spring and ♂♂ then take up territories but pairs are not formed. The
displaying cock presents a remarkable spectacle: it lays its head on its
back, inflates a special sac in its throat and droops its wings, also displaying the white under-surfaces of wings and tail; at the same time it
squats almost to the ground and quivers its wings. The 2–3, occasionally
4 olive-green, brown-blotched eggs are incubated by the ♀ for close on
4 weeks. The ♂ takes no interest in the brood, associating with other ♂♂
at this time. The young stay with the ♀ until autumn. The ♂♂ then join
such parties, and flocks stay united through the winter. Single-brooded.

Food: Green plantmatter, seeds, insects, worms, small vertebrates (frogs,
mice etc.).

Little Bustard · *Otis tetrax* L. (Illustration follows p. 151, below)

Family: Bustards (Otididae)

Description: The breeding-plumage ♂ is sandy-brown above with fine
dark vermiculations and has black primaries and grey secondaries. Its
head is grey and its neck black with a sort of white "necklace"; at the
base of the neck is a white band, and below this a black one. Its breast
and belly are white. In winter plumage it resembles the ♀ but still has

Little Ringed Plover · *Charadrius dubius* (p. 166) Above

Ringed Plover · *Charadrius hiaticula* (p. 166) Below

unflecked flanks. The ♀ is mainly brown with blackish barring and streaking; her underparts are whitish with dark brown spotting, particularly on the flanks. Juveniles are like the ♀. L: 17″, Wt: c. 2 lb.

The displaying ♂ produces loud snorting calls like "krerr krerr".

Distribution: The Mediterranean region, locally in France and Belgium, southeast Europe, eastwards to the central Asiatic steppes. A partial migrant, European birds wintering mainly in the Mediterranean area. *Habitat:* Dry open country, open farmland.

Breeding: It may breed when 2 years old. The ♂ displays on special, generally raised or open spots. It ruffles its neck-feathers, fans its tail and droops its wings. The 3–4 olive-brown eggs, laid in a shallow scrape, hatch after about 3 weeks' incubation by the ♀ alone. She keeps charge of the young until they are able to fly at 5 weeks. Single-brooded. *Food:* Proportionately more animal matter than is taken by the Great Bustard.

Oystercatcher · *Haematopus ostralegus* L. (Illustration precedes p. 154)

Family: Oystercatchers (Haematopodidae)
Description: The upper parts, head, neck and breast are black; the belly, rump and front part of the tail, and a band along the wings are white. Bill and legs are red. A white band crosses the throat in winter. Juveniles are like winter-plumage adults. L: 17″, Wt: c. 18 oz.

Its shrill, penetrating "klee-eep" is varied almost into a trill in the piping display. Sharp "pick-pick..." calls denote excitement.

Distribution: The entire European coastline, except for parts of the Mediterranean (also breeding inland along river valleys in northern Britain); by the Black Sea and over a large area of west central Asia; coasts of North and South America, also east Asia, South Africa, Australia and New Zealand. It is mainly resident.

Kentish Plover · *Charadrius alexandrinus* (p. 167) ♂ Above ▷

Dotterel · *Eudromias morinellus* (p. 170) Below ▷

159

Habitat: Mud-flats, sandy and rocky shores, sand-dunes; in some areas also riverside shingle-banks and farmland. Large flocks occur where food is plentiful.

Breeding: Sexually mature at 3 years. The nest-scrape may be in shingle, sand, soil or on a ledge of rock and is lined with shells and pebbles if available. The eggs, most often 3, are grey-buff with blackish spots (good camouflage on shingle) and are incubated by ♂ and ♀ for *c.* 27 days. The downy young leave the nest when a day old and remain in the area, the parents bringing food. The fledging period is about 5 weeks. Single-brooded.

Food: Mussels and other molluscs, marine worms, crustaceans, insects.

Spur-winged Plover · *Vanellus spinosus* (L.)
(Illustration follows p. 155, above)

Family: Plovers (Charadriidae)

Description: The back is sandy-brown; the neck, apart from a narrow black stripe down the front, is white. Crown, breast, belly and tail are black. The under tail-coverts and rump are white. There is a small spur at the bend of each wing. Juveniles are more brownish. L: 10½″, Wt: *c.* 6 oz.

Metallic sounding "pitt-pitt…" calls are given by this species.

Distribution: North Greece, Turkey, Cyprus, the eastern Mediterranean coast, Africa. It is a summer visitor, wintering in Africa.

Habitat: Open, flat country with sparse vegetation, especially in the region of large river-estuaries.

Breeding: Birds may become sexually mature at 1 year. Nest: a scrape lined with a little vegetation. The normally 4 eggs, olive-brown with dark spots, are brooded by both partners for about 3 weeks. The young follow their parents from the nest when they are dry, and remain with them until autumn. Single-brooded.

Food: Insects and their larvae, molluscs, worms.

Turnstone · *Arenaria interpres* (p. 171) Above

Golden Plover · *Pluvialis apricaria* (p. 174) in breeding plumage Below

Allied species: The slightly larger Sociable Plover (*Chettusia gregaria*) breeds in south Russia and the steppes of central Asia. It is largely pale grey-brown with a black crown, white stripe over and black stripe through the eye. Its white tail has a black band near the tip.

Lapwing (Peewit) · *Vanellus vanellus* (L.)
(Illustration follows p. 155, below)

Family: Plovers (Charadriidae)
Description: ♂ and ♀ are dark green on the back (looking black at a distance) with purplish gloss on the wing-coverts and black, white-tipped primaries. The crown, forehead, throat, neck and upper breast are black; the rest of the underside, apart from the rusty under tail-coverts, are white. A slender crest arises at the back of the head. Juveniles are duller, with only a hint of the crest. L: 12″, Wt: *c.* 7 oz.

The name "peewit" well describes the bird's call. During spring-display calls like "peeer-weet-weet-weet..." may be heard.

Distribution: Most of Europe, but absent from the far north and many Mediterranean areas; it extends right across Asia. A partial migrant in Europe, it winters in the British Isles, mid-, west and south Europe, also North Africa. Lapwings usually migrate and feed in flocks.
Habitat: Marshy and other meadows with shortish vegetation, arable fields, moorland, sewage farms, muddy shores in winter.

Breeding: Sexually mature at 1 year. Spectacular tumbling display-flights are performed in spring. ♂ and ♀ make several scrapes, one of which is lined with a few straws, and here the 4 olive, dark-blotched eggs are laid. Incubation, by both partners, takes 24–31 days. The well-camouflaged mottled brownish and white downy chicks leave the nest soon after drying and are tended by the parents. They begin flying after about 35 days. Single-brooded. Lapwings often breed socially.
Food: Molluscs, worms, insects and their larvae, weed-seeds.

Golden Plover · *Pluvialis apricaria* (p. 174) in winter plumage ▷

Little Ringed Plover · *Charadrius dubius* Scop.
(Illustration precedes p. 158, above)

Family: Plovers (Charadriidae)
Description: The upperparts are sandy with a white forehead, above
which is a black band joined to the broad black eyestripe. The chin and
a ring round the neck are white and below this is a black ring. The
underparts are otherwise white; the wings are uniformly sandy-grey.
There is a bare, pale yellow ring round the eye, the bill is blackish, and
the legs are flesh-coloured. Juveniles lack the black head-markings and
have only very incomplete throat-bands. L: 6″, Wt: *c.* 1½ oz.

   The call-note is a piping "diu"; when agitated a sharp "gigigigig" is
uttered. In the breeding season the ♂ gives a soft trill during display-
flights.

Distribution: Europe (except for Iceland, Ireland, Wales, most of Scot-
land and much of Scandinavia); Asia, the East Indies, Madeira, the
Canaries, North Africa. Most birds winter in Africa.
Habitat: Gravel- and sand-pits, shingle by fresh water, sewage farms.

Breeding: It breeds when 1 year old. The nest scrape is formed in any
bare, loose surface, and lined with pebbles, small shells etc. The usually
4 eggs, greyish-buff with dark spots, are incubated by ♂ and ♀ for
22–26 days. The young run from the scrape soon after hatching, and
follow the parents. They can fly after about 3 weeks. Often double-
brooded.
Food: Insects, larvae, spiders, small crustaceans, snails.

Ringed Plover · *Charadrius hiaticula* L.
(Illustration precedes p. 158, below)

Family: Plovers (Charadriidae)
Description: In breeding plumage ♂ and ♀ resemble the little ringed
plover but have orangy bills with black tips, orange eye-rings and

Woodcock · *Scolopax rusticola* (p. 175) Above

Snipe · *Gallinago gallinago* (p. 175) Below

orange-yellow legs, and a white wing-bar which shows in flight. The black markings become more brownish in winter. Juveniles are, apart from the wing-bar, similar to those of the last species. L: 7½", Wt: *c*. 2 oz.

Ringed plovers often occur in small parties. The call is a musical "tooeep".

Distribution: The coasts of the British Isles, east side of the North Sea and the Baltic; Scandinavia, northeast Europe, Spitzbergen, Iceland, Greenland, Baffin Land, northern Asia. A partial migrant, it winters in west and south Europe.
Habitat: Sandy and shingly shorelines, mudflats; over much of the range (including north Britain) it also breeds inland by rivers, lakes, even on tundra.

Breeding: Much as for the little ringed plover. ♂ and ♀ incubate the usually 4 greyish-buff, dark-spotted eggs (which, like those of other plovers, blend beautifully with the typical surrounding terrain) for *c*. 23–27 days. Single- or double-brooded.
Food: Insects and their larvae, crustaceans, molluscs.

Kentish Plover · *Charadrius alexandrinus* L.
(Illustration follows p. 159, above)

Family: Plovers (Charadriidae)
Description: The ♂ plumage-pattern resembles that of the last two species but there is no black "collar", just a black patch on each "shoulder". Juveniles and ♀ have brown, not black markings. ♂ and ♀ have blackish bill and legs. L: 6¼", Wt: *c*. 1½ oz.

Voice: a musical "pooit", and "tirr". The ♂ trills during the bat-like display-flight. Agitated birds call "tiup tiup tiup".

Distribution: The coast of continental Europe, except the north; salt-steppe areas near Lake Neusiedl (Austria); saline lakes and coasts of Africa, Asia, Australia, southern North America, the Antilles. A partial

Curlew · *Numenius arquata* (p. 178) ▷

migrant in Europe, it winters mainly in the Mediterranean region. It is
an uncommon visitor to Britain, and no longer breeds in Kent!
Habitat: Chiefly coastal: sand, pebbles or mud-flats; also salt-steppes,
saline lakes and sandbanks by rivers.

Breeding and *Food:* Details resemble those for ringed plover; however
the normal clutch is 3 eggs, stone-buff with dark streaks and spots.

Dotterel · *Eudromias morinellus* (L.) (Illustration follows p. 159, below)

Family: Plovers (Charadriidae)
Description: Breeding plumage is grey-brown above with buff feather-
edging and the crown dark brown. White stripes above each eye meet
on the nape. The pale brownish-grey upper breast is separated from the
chestnut lower breast by a white band. The belly is blackish, under tail-
coverts are white. Winter and juvenile plumage are duller and lack black
on the belly. L: $8\frac{1}{2}$", Wt: *c.* 4 oz.

The birds produce soft "dirrit" and "diwirree" calls. A warning note
when alarmed is "hooee". Trills are uttered during display-flights.

Distribution: North Scotland, rarely north England, in Holland recently,
Scandinavia, the Apennines, eastern Alps, northwest Czechoslovakia, the
Carpathians, Urals, Asia and Alaska. European breeders winter in the
southeast Mediterranean area, by the Red Sea, in deserts by the Persian
Gulf.
Habitat: Treeless tundra, mountain plateaux above the tree-limit, in the
far north moors with low vegetation. A few have recently bred at sea-
level on Dutch polders. Outside the breeding season it occurs by water,
on fields, in semi-desert and salt-steppe country.

Breeding: It breeds when 1 year old. A shallow scrape between stones or
very low plant tussocks serves as nest. It is the ♂ that incubates the
mostly 3 olive-brown, heavily blotched blackish eggs; they hatch after
c. $3\frac{1}{2}$ weeks. The ♀ takes no interest in either the clutch or the brood.
Single-brooded.

Whimbrel · *Numenius phaeopus* (p. 179)

Food: Insects and their larvae, worms, snails; sometimes also berries and green plant matter.

Turnstone · *Arenaria interpres* (L.) (Illustration precedes p. 162, above)

Family: Plovers (Charadriidae)
Description: Breeding plumage is chestnut above with black markings, white below with a black "bib"; the face shows bold white and black patterning. In winter plumage the upperparts are dark grey-brown, the throat is whitish, the breast-band grey-brown. Juvenile plumage is similar. L: 9″, Wt: *c.* 3½ oz.

It is not very vocal; a staccato "kick-e-kick" or "kikikikikik" is used in flight, and "tchick-tchick-tchick..." when agitated. The mating song is an ever-quickening sequence of "tchewick-tchewick" and similar notes.

Distribution: The coasts of northern Europe, northern Asia, North America, Greenland; outside the breeding season coasts all over the world.
Habitat: Coasts with pebbly or low rocky ground and scanty plant-life, tundra with low vegetation, river-mouths, small grassy islands. In winter it prefers beaches with seaweed-covered rocks.

Breeding: Sexual maturity may only be reached at 3 years; hence many birds in breeding dress summer in west Europe, the tropics and the southern Hemisphere. At the start of the breeding season ♂♂ perform reeling display-flights and sing over their territories. Courtship-chases of the ♀♀ also occur. The 3–4 greyish-olive, brown-blotched eggs are laid in a scrape made in the ground. Incubation is by ♂ and ♀, lasting somewhat over 3 weeks. Single-brooded.
Food: Shellfish, crustaceans, insects (especially in summer) etc., also tundra plants and seeds. Sandhoppers are found by turning over stones. Carrion and scraps are also eaten at times.

Black-tailed Godwit · *Limosa limosa* (p. 182) ▷

Golden Plover · *Pluvialis apricaria* (L.)
(Illustrations precede p. 162, below, and follow p. 163)

Family: Plovers (Charadriidae)
Description: The breeding plumage is dark above with golden yellow flecking, the forehead and a stripe above the eye being white. The face and underside are to a greater or lesser degree black in summer, but are pale in winter and in juvenile plumage. L: 11″, Wt: *c.* 7 oz.

The call is a piping "tluee", which in the song becomes a trill sounding like "trlutioo-trlutioo…". Display-flight is accompanied by a mournful "phew-pheeoo…".

Distribution: Iceland, the Faeroes, northern and western parts of the British Isles, north Germany (rare), Scandinavia, northeast Europe and northwest Siberia. A partial migrant, it winters in west Europe and the Mediterranean region.
Habitat: Moors with short vegetation, arctic heathland. Outside the breeding season fields, saltings and mudflats.

Breeding: It possibly breeds when a year old. The ♂ performs display-flights with slow wing-beats over the breeding grounds, accompanied by calling. The eggs, usually 3–4, are buffish with blackish-brown blotches. Incubation, by ♂ and ♀, takes about 27 days. Single-brooded.

Food: Insects and their larvae, molluscs, worms, spiders, sometimes also green plant matter, berries and seeds.

Allied species: The slightly larger Grey Plover (*P. squatarola*) has white and grey flecking above; it loses its black face and belly in winter but retains black "armpits" visible when the wings are raised. It breeds in extreme northeast Europe, arctic Asia and North America, wintering on muddy shores of many regions.

Bar-tailed Godwit · *Limosa lapponica* (p. 183) Above

Wood Sandpiper · *Tringa glareola* (p. 183) Below

Woodcock · *Scolopax rusticola* L. (Illustration precedes p. 166, above)

Family: Sandpipers, snipe, etc. (Scolopacidae)
Description: The back is warm brown, cryptically patterned with light and dark markings. The back of the head is dark with pale cross-bands. There is dark barring on the light brown underparts. Juveniles are similar. L: 13½", Wt: *c.* 12 oz.

During its display-flight at dusk and dawn, known as "roding", the ♂ makes a croaking "kworkwork" and a bleating "quitz" which usually follows the croak.

Distribution: Europe, except for the Iberian peninsula, the northeast and north Scandinavia; only Corsica in the Mediterranean region. Temperate Asia, Madeira, the Azores and Canaries. It is a partial migrant in Europe, wintering in western and Mediterranean regions.
Habitat: Open woodland with clearings up to the tree-limit.

Breeding: Sexually mature at 1 year. In spring the ♂ makes "roding" flights over its territory and drives off other ♂♂. Ground-display involves drooping the wings and erecting and spreading the tail. After mating the ♂ takes no more interest in the ♀, which generally lays 4 eggs, light buff with darker markings, in a scrape lined with dry leaves and moss, and incubates them for 20–23 days. Single- or double-brooded.
Food: Worms, insects and their larvae, small crustaceans.

Snipe · *Gallinago gallinago* (L.) (Illustration precedes p. 166, below)

Family: Sandpipers, snipe, etc. (Scolopacidae)
Description: ♂ and ♀ appear dark brown above with creamy-buff stripes down the back. The blackish-brown crown has a buff, lengthwise central stripe; a similar stripe lies above each eye. The breast is buff with dark flecking, the rest of the underparts are whitish. Juvenile dress is similar. L: 10½", Wt: *c.* 4 oz.

Common Sandpiper · *Tringa hypoleucos* (p. 186) ▷

During spring display-flights the ♂ produces a "drumming" sound, considered to be made by vibration in the air of the outer tail feathers. The song sounds like "chip-per...chip-per...". Flushed birds utter a rasping "scaap".

Distribution: Europe, but almost absent from Mediterranean countries; large stretches of Asia, east and south Africa, North and South America. Partially migrant in Europe, it winters in western and Mediterranean areas.

Habitat: Marshy meadows, rushy bogs, boggy moorland; outside the breeding season also by water with muddy shallows, and on sewage farms etc.

Breeding: Sexually mature at 1 year. The nest scrape, hidden in a tussock, is lined with grasses. The 4 olive-brown, dark-blotched eggs are incubated by the ♀ alone, for 20–21 days. Single- or double-brooded.

Food: Largely worms, also insects, snails, some plant-seeds.

Allied species: The larger, but similar Great Snipe (*G. media*) has much white on the sides of the tail. It breeds in northwest Scandinavia, northeast Europe and west Siberia.

The small Jack Snipe (*Lymnocryptes minimus*) has a less long bill and has two conspicuous creamy stripes down the length of the purplish-glossed back. It rarely rises until almost trodden on, then flies straight, not zig-zagging as the snipe does. It nests in north Scandinavia, northeast Europe and Siberia, moving south in winter.

Curlew · *Numenius arquata* (L.) (Illustration follows p. 167)

Family: Sandpipers, snipe, etc. (Scolopacidae)

Description: The head and neck are light brown with grey-brown streaks; the back is more heavily marked with blackish-brown. The underparts are grey-white with dark shaft-streaks. The lower back and rump are white; the tail is barred whitish and grey-brown. The bill is long and down-curved. Juvenile plumage resembles the adult's. L: *c.* 22″, Wt: *c.* 28 oz.

Greenshank · *Tringa nebularia* (p. 187)

Voice: a musical "coorlee", which in the song is speeded up into a bubbling trill. Anxiety note: a barking "kwickickick".

Distribution: Europe (except Iceland, the Mediterranean region and the northeast); Asia. A partial migrant, it winters in west and south Europe and in Africa.
Habitat: Moorland with reasonably short vegetation, upland pastures, rushy meadows, lowland bogs. Outside the breeding season it occurs mainly on coasts, often in flocks.

Breeding: Sexually mature at 1–2 years. In spring the ♂♂ make bubbling song-flights. In ground-display the ♂ makes tripping steps round the ♀, bowing, spreading its wings and showing its white rump. The nest-hollow is scraped out and lined with any nearby grasses. The usually 4 eggs are greenish- or brownish-olive with dark markings. ♂ and ♀ take turns incubating for about 4 weeks. The young are tended by both partners for about 6 weeks. Single-brooded.
Food: Worms, snails, insects and their larvae, crustaceans, small frogs and fish, also berries and seeds.

Whimbrel · *Numenius phaeopus* (L.) (Illustration precedes p. 170)

Family: Sandpipers, snipe, etc. (Scolopacidae)
Description: Rather like a small edition of the curlew; the crown is blackish-brown with a creamy streak along the centre, and there is a pale stripe over the eye. The bill is shorter. L: *c.* 16″, Wt: *c.* 12 oz.
   Call: a whinnying "tititititi". The song resembles the curlew's.

Distribution: Iceland, the Faeroes, the Shetland Is. (rarely elsewhere in North Scotland), Scandinavia, northeast Europe, Siberia, Alaska and north Canada. It is a summer visitor, wintering in tropical parts of Africa, South America and southern Asia.

Redshank · *Tringa totanus* (p. 190) Above ▷

Dunlin · *Calidris alpina* (p. 191) Below ▷

Habitat: Moorland with usually short vegetation, sometimes marshy ground. Coastal outside the breeding season, but it may be seen over inland places on passage.

Breeding and *Food:* Broadly as for curlew.

Black-tailed Godwit · *Limosa limosa* (L.) (Illustration follows p. 171)

Family: Sandpipers, snipe, etc. (Scolopacidae)
Description: In breeding dress the back is blackish-brown with rufous feather-edges; the head and neck are predominantly chestnut, the wings black with a broad white bar which shows in flight. The breast is chestnut, the belly and flanks are off-white with dark barring. Upper and under tail-coverts are white, the tail is black. The long bill has only a suggestion of an upward tilt. The chestnut parts become grey in winter plumage. Juveniles are like a pale ♀ but with a whitish belly. L: *c.* 16″, Wt: *c.* 9 oz.

An almost lapwing-like "kweeit" and a sharp "gritta" may be heard from the birds. During display-flights the ♂ yodels "dileedyo-dileedyo-leedyo-leedyo-...".

Distribution: Iceland, the British Isles (very rare but increasing), mid- and west Europe, particularly in coastal regions, south Sweden and Denmark, also east Europe and Asia. A partial migrant in Europe, it winters in the west, the Mediterranean area and Africa.
Habitat: Marshy ground, water-meadows, sometimes heathland. Outside the breeding season it frequents coastal mudflats, also muddy margins of inland waters.

Breeding: Sexually mature at 1 year. In the ground-display the ♂ struts round the ♀ with its fanned tail depressed at a steep angle. The eggs (generally 4) are pear-shaped, greenish- or brownish-olive with dark

Little Stint · *Calidris minuta* (p. 194) Above

Ruff · *Philomachus pugnax* (p. 195) ♀ Below

brown blotches. They are laid in a scrape lined with grasses and leaves, and incubated by both partners for about 24 days. The young can fly after 5 weeks. Single-brooded.

Food: Insects and their larvae, worms, molluscs, crustaceans, tadpoles and spawn of amphibia.

Bar-tailed Godwit · *Limosa lapponica* (L.)
(Illustration precedes p. 174, above)

Family: Sandpipers, snipe, etc. (Scolopacidae)
Description: It resembles the black-tailed godwit, but has chestnut underparts and a white tail with grey barring, no wing-bar, and shorter legs; the bill is distinctly upturned. The ♀ is paler. Juveniles are like ♀♀ but more streaked. Winter plumage shows grey-brown mottling above, pale sandy, faintly streaked breast and white belly. L: *c.* 15″, Wt: *c.* 8½ oz.

It has a harsh "gyegegegeg" call and a shrill "krick" if alarmed. The display-song is like the yodelling of the black-tailed godwit in form.

Distribution: North Scandinavia and northeast Europe, northern Asia and west Alaska. European birds winter on the southern North Sea coast and around the British Isles, by the Mediterranean, in tropical Africa and southeast Asia.
Habitat: Tundra and marshy ground in the far north. Outside the breeding season it favours muddy or sandy shores (where non-breeders may also summer), rarely occurring inland.

Breeding and *Food:* As for the black-tailed godwit.

Wood Sandpiper · *Tringa glareola* L.
(Illustration precedes p. 174, below)

Family: Sandpipers, snipe, etc. (Scolopacidae)
Description: The upperparts are dark brown with white spots; the rump and upper tail-coverts are white; the tail has about 6 dark bars. The

Ruff · *Philomachus pugnax* (p. 195) ♂♂ displaying ▷

underside is white with a greyish-brown tinge and dark streaking on the throat and neck. There is a white stripe above the eye. The legs are greenish-yellow. L: *c*. 8″, Wt: *c*. 2½ oz.

Flushed birds utter a shrill "chiff-chiffchiff-...". The song, given during display-flight, is a musical "teedlteedlteedlteedl...".

Distribution: North Germany, Scandinavia, northeast Europe, northern Asia. A few have recently bred in north Scotland. It is a summer visitor to Europe, wintering mainly in tropical and southern Africa, a minority by the Mediterranean.

Habitat: Heathland, usually marshy, open swampy woodland in the north; outside the breeding season on muddy patches by fresh water, sewage farms.

Breeding: Sexually mature at 1 year. The nest is a sparsely-lined hollow in a sheltered spot on the ground. The usually 4 eggs are pale olive-green or buff with chocolate blotches; they are ovate. Incubation, by ♂ and ♀, takes around 3 weeks. The young become independent after 5 weeks. Single-brooded.

Food: Insects and their larvae, spiders, molluscs and worms.

Allied species: The similar Green Sandpiper (*T. ochropus*) is a little bigger, darker above and under the wings, and has more white on the tail. It breeds in Scandinavia, east Europe and large areas of Asia.

Common Sandpiper · *Tringa hypoleucos* L.
(Illustration follows p. 175)

Family: Sandpipers, snipe, etc. (Scolopacidae)
Description: The upperparts are grey-brown with a pale stripe over the eye. The underparts are white with diffuse brownish streaking on the sides of the breast. Winter and juvenile plumage are similar to breeding plumage. L: 8″, Wt: 1½–1¾ oz.

Notes similar to the shrill "tweedeedee" call make up the trill uttered during song-flight.

Distribution: Nearly all of Europe and large parts of Asia, North America. It is largely a summer visitor to Europe, wintering in Africa and south Asia with small numbers also in mid- and south Europe.

Habitat: Shingly or rocky banks of clear-flowing rivers, streams and lakes to above the tree-limit. Mainly by fresh water on passage.

Breeding: Sexually mature at 1 year. During ground-display the birds trip back and forth with fanned and downward-flicked tail. The nest-scrape, near or some way from water, may be under herbage or fairly exposed. The 4 creamy-buff, dark-spotted eggs are incubated by ♂ and ♀ for about 3 weeks. The young are independent at about 4 weeks. Single-brooded.
Food: Insects and their larvae, molluscs, crustaceans.

Greenshank · *Tringa nebularia* (Gunn.) (Illustration precedes p. 178)

Family: Sandpipers, snipe, etc. (Scolopacidae)
Description: The wings are dark grey-brown, the lower back, rump and upper tail-coverts white, and the head and neck off-white with grey-brown streaking. The underside is white from the breast rearwards. The legs are greenish. Winter plumage is paler; juveniles show buff feather-edgings on the wing-coverts and the upper back. L: *c.* 12″, Wt: *c.* 6 oz.
  Voice: "tewtewtew"; in song-flight a rapidly repeated "deeheedl-deeheedl…".

Distribution: North Scotland, Scandinavia (except for the southwest), northeast Europe, large stretches of Asia. It is a summer visitor, wintering mainly in tropical Africa, and also in the Mediterranean area (and a few in the British Isles).
Habitat: Greenshanks feed by lochs and nest on nearby moorland or in forest-clearings. On passage they visit coastal mud-flats, reservoirs and sewage farms.

Breeding: Sexual maturity is possibly attained at 1 year. The ♂ utters its rich flute-like notes during undulating song-flights, and swerving sexual chases occur. The nest-scrape, lined with handy plant material, is often by a rock or dead log. The 4 eggs are buff with dark spots or blotches;

Avocet · *Recurvirostra avosetta* (p. 198) ▷

incubation by ♂ and ♀ takes *c.* 3½ weeks. The young become independent at around 5 weeks. Single-brooded.

Food: Insects, crustaceans, worms, molluscs, spiders.

Allied species: The breeding plumage of the Spotted Redshank (*T. erythropus*) is sooty black with white-speckled upperparts, dark red legs and dark bill. It breeds in north Scandinavia, northeast Europe and Siberia.

The Marsh Sandpiper (*T. stagnatilis*), which resembles a small Greenshank, breeds in southeast Europe and Asia.

The Terek Sandpiper (*T. terek*) has a curious long, lightly upcurved bill, 2 black stripes down the back, grey rump and brown tail; it breeds in northeast Europe and Siberia.

Redshank · *Tringa totanus* L. (Illustration follows p. 179, above)

Family: Sandpipers, snipe, etc. (Scolopacidae)

Description: The crown and back are brown with darker markings; the sides of the head, throat, neck and breast are off-white with dark streaking; the remaining underparts, lower back and rump are white. The upper tail-coverts and tail are white with dark barring. It has orange-red legs and a reddish, black-tipped bill. Juveniles have more dark markings; adults in winter are paler. The white wing-bars are conspicuous in flight. L: 11″, Wt: *c.* 4½ oz.

The call is a piping "tyududu", a high "chip-chip-chip…" shows agitation. The song, in flight, is a melodious "deedldeedldeedl…".

Distribution: Iceland, the British Isles, Scandinavia, north-central and eastern Europe, Asia; local on the French coast, in Iberia and Italy. A partial migrant in Europe it winters in the west and the Mediterranean region.

Habitat: Water-meadows, damp moorland, saltings. It winters mainly along muddy bays and estuaries.

Breeding and *Food:* In the spring the ♂ makes "yodelling" display-flights. The nest is in a grass or rushy tussock. Otherwise details are as for greenshank.

Black-winged Stilt · *Himantopus himantopus* (p. 198)

190

Dunlin · *Calidris alpina* (L.) (Illustration follows p. 179, below)

Family: Sandpipers, snipe, etc. (Scolopacidae)
Description: In breeding dress the upperparts are rich brown with dark streaking, the underparts whitish with streaking on neck and throat; the lower breast and belly are black. There is a pale eyestripe. The white wing-bar and sides to the tail show in flight. The bill is faintly downcurved. Winter plumage is grey-brown above with darker and lighter scaling, white below with grey throat-streaks. Juveniles are similar to this but have a browner tinge. L: 7″, Wt: *c.* 1½ oz.

Whirring notes are uttered like "trirr" and "skree". Agitated birds call "weeweewee". The ♂ trills during display-flight.

Distribution: Northwest Europe (including west and north Britain and Ireland), Scandinavia, the Baltic coast, Spitzbergen, north Asia, Greenland, arctic North America. A partial migrant, it winters around coasts of west Europe and the Mediterranean, sometimes in flocks numbering thousands.
Habitat: Bogs and moorland with pools, mossy tundra, sometimes marshy grassland, saltmarshes; outside the breeding season especially on muddy shores (where some non-breeders summer), also shallows by fresh water, sewage farms etc.

Breeding: Sexually mature at 1 year. The nest-hollow is mostly formed in a concealing grass tussock. ♂ and ♀ brood the 4 olive-buff eggs with dark brown blotches for *c.* 3 weeks. The young are independent by 6 weeks. Single-brooded.
Food: Insects, crustaceans, worms, molluscs, some plant matter.

Allied species: The Curlew Sandpiper (*C. ferruginea*), rather like a dunlin but with white upper tail-coverts, breeds in arctic Asia and occurs in Europe only on passage.

The larger Knot (*C. canutus*) has the underparts brick-red in summer, white with fine streaking in winter. Breeding in Spitzbergen, Greenland,

Red-necked Phalarope · *Phalaropus lobatus* (p. 199) Above ▷

Stone Curlew · *Burhinus oedicnemus* (p. 202) Below ▷

arctic North America, northwest Siberia and islands in the Arctic Ocean; many birds winter on west European coasts, at times in huge flocks.

Little Stint · *Calidris minuta* (Leisl.)
(Illustration precedes p. 182, above)

Family: Sandpipers, snipe, etc. (Scolopacidae)
Description: The breeding plumage is rufous with dark markings and light feather-edging above, pale below. Winter plumage is grey-brown above, whitish below. Juveniles are black-brown above with warm buff feather-edging, whitish below with light buff on the breast; the light markings on the back produce the effect of a rearward-pointing "V". The central upper tail-coverts and tail feathers are dark, the sides of the tail light grey. L: 5¼", Wt: *c.* 1 oz.

The species makes a clinking "dirrididit". A rising and falling trill accompanies display by the ♂.

Distribution: Northeast Europe, north Siberia. It is a summer visitor which winters largely in tropical and southern Africa and in south Asia.
Habitat: Tundra with mainly short vegetation; outside the breeding season muddy water-margins, sewage farms.

Breeding and *Food:* Much as for dunlin.

Allied species: The similar Temminck's Stint (*C. temminckii*) has no pale "V" on the back; it has white sides to the tail. It breeds in north Scandinavia, northeast Europe and Siberia.

The Purple Sandpiper (*C. maritima*) is largely slate-grey, but has pale feather-margins in summer; it breeds in Iceland, the Faeroes, north Scandinavia, locally in the Holarctic, and winters as far south as Britain, feeding among seaweed at the tide's edge.

In summer the Sanderling (*Crocethia alba*) is a black-streaked chestnut above and on the throat with a white belly; in winter it appears almost

Pratincole · *Glareola pratincola* (p. 203) Above

Great Skua (Bonxie) · *Stercorarius skua* (p. 203) Below

white (being in fact pale grey above). It runs along the sand like a clockwork toy. Breeding in Spitzbergen, Greenland, arctic America, Siberia; some winter on west European coasts.

The Broad-billed Sandpiper (*Limicola falcinellus*), dark brown above with pale markings and 2 white lines over each eye, breeds in north Scandinavia and Siberia.

Ruff · *Philomachus pugnax* (L.)
(Illustrations precede p. 182, below, and follow p. 183)

Family: Sandpipers, snipe, etc. (Scolopacidae)
Description: In breeding plumage ♂♂ have a scaly pattern of blackish and buff above and a remarkable ruff around the neck, varying in colour from bird to bird. They have a dark breast, white belly and under tail-coverts. In winter plumage the ♂ resembles the considerably smaller ♀, lacking a ruff. There is an oval white patch each side of the tail; the bill is rather short. Juveniles resemble the ♀. L: ♂ *c.* 11½″, ♀ *c.* 9″; Wt: ♂ *c.* 7 oz, ♀ *c.* 4½ oz.

A rather silent species; occasionally a "gehgehgeh" may be heard.

Distribution: The Atlantic coast of France, coastal regions of the North Sea and Baltic, Scandinavia, east Europe, Siberia. (Small numbers now breed again in long-abandoned haunts in east England.) It winters in coastal regions of west Europe and the Mediterranean, and in Africa.
Habitat: Low-lying meadows, tundra, fresh-water lakes, salt-marshes and brackish lagoons with marshy ground around. On passage it favours muddy water-margins and sewage farms.

Breeding: Sexually mature at 1 year. Soon after reaching the breeding areas, ♂♂ assemble at special display-grounds, each picking a mound from which he drives off rivals. Some ♀♀ are always to be found in the vicinity of these display-grounds, where one of the dominant cocks "treads" them. The ♂♂ take no interest in eggs or broods. The ♀ forms

Great Black-backed Gull · *Larus marinus* (p. 206) Above ▷

Herring Gull · *Larus argentatus* (p. 207) Below ▷

a scrape, lines it with grass and lays 4 olive-green eggs, blotched with dark brown, which take 21 days to hatch. The young become independent in about 6 weeks. Single-brooded.
Food: Insects, small crustaceans, worms, molluscs.

Avocet · *Recurvirostra avosetta* L. (Illustration follows p. 187)

Family: Avocets (Recurvirostridae)
Description: The upper part of the head and back of the neck, wing-tips, wing-bar and sides of the back are black; the remaining plumage is white. The legs are blue-grey. The bill is markedly upturned. In juveniles the black areas are brownish. L: 17″, Wt: *c.* 12 oz.
   Voice: a musical "klooit"; when agitated a hard "klipit klipit...".

Distribution: Coastal areas of Holland, Denmark, Germany, south Scandinavia, east England (Suffolk); locally by the Mediterranean, in west France and southeast central Europe, southeast Europe, Asia, Africa. A partial migrant in Europe, it winters largely in the Mediterranean area (a few in S. England).
Habitat: Margins of brackish or saline lagoons with scant vegetation, salt-marshes, seacoasts.

Breeding: It may become sexually mature at 1 year, and often breeds colonially. The nest-hollow, lined with a few plant-stems, is on bare ground or short grass. ♂ and ♀ incubate the 3–4 clay-coloured, black-spotted eggs for *c.* 24–25 days. The young are fully grown at about 6 weeks. Single-brooded.
Food: Small shrimps, plankton, molluscs, insects.

Black-winged Stilt · *Himantopus himantopus* (L.) (Ill. precedes p. 190)

Family: Avocets (Recurvirostridae)
Description: The plumage is white apart from black back and wings. The very long red legs trail far beyond the tail in flight. The bill is straight and dark. ♂♂ have a dark zone on the back of the head; ♀♀ have

Lesser Black-backed Gull · *Larus fuscus* (p. 210)

white heads. Juveniles resemble adults but have the back of the head grey-brown. L: 15″, Wt: *c.* 6 oz.

The call is a shrill "kip kip...".

Distribution: Southwest Europe, locally in the Mediterranean area, southeast Europe, Asia, Australia, New Zealand, locally in Africa, Madagascar, southern North America, Central and South America. In Britain it is a rare visitor, but has bred. European birds are summer visitors, wintering mainly in tropical Africa.
Habitat: Fresh-water and brackish pools and lagoons with muddy banks and extensive shallows, Salicornia-flats, marshy meadows, rice-paddies.

Breeding: Much as for avocet, although nests may be in shallow water.
Food: Insects and their larvae, molluscs, worms, crustaceans, tadpoles, perhaps also small fish.

Red-necked Phalarope · *Phalaropus lobatus* (L.) (Illustration follows p. 191, above)

Family: Phalaropes (Phalaropodidae)
Description: Breeding plumage is dark greyish above with buff feather-edges; the chin is white, the neck rusty red, the remaining underparts whitish. (♀♀ are brighter than ♂♂.) Winter plumage is slate-grey above, white below, with a white forehead and dark stripe through the eye. Juveniles resemble winter adults but are browner. The needle-like bill is dark; the feet are lobed for swimming. L: 7″, Wt: *c.* 1½ oz.

The call-note is a short "tchritt".

Distribution: Iceland, the Faeroes, some N. Scottish islands (very rare in mainland Scotland and Ireland), Scandinavia, east Europe, Siberia, North America, Spitzbergen, Greenland. It is a summer visitor, spending the winter out on the Indian and South Atlantic Oceans.
Habitat: Lakes and pools with vegetated shallows, wet marshes. It may turn up on any type of water on passage.

Common Gull · *Larus canus* (p. 211) Above ▷

Slender-billed Gull · *Larus genei* (p. 211) Below ▷

Breeding: Sexually mature at 1 year, it nests in grass tussocks. The 4 olive-buff eggs are incubated entirely by the ♂ (which also tends the young) for *c.* 3 weeks. Single-brooded.
Food: Insects and aquatic larvae, small crustaceans.

Allied species: The Grey Phalarope (*P. fulicarius*) is stouter, and in summer is rufous below with white cheeks. In winter it is like *P. lobatus* in colour but the thicker bill is yellowish. It breeds in Iceland, Spitzbergen, Novaya Zemlaya, arctic Asia and North America, and winters at sea.

Stone Curlew · *Burhinus oedicnemus* (L.)
(Illustration follows p. 191, below)

Family: Thick-knees (Burhinidae)
Description: The upperparts are light grey-brown with darker streaking. The underparts are whitish, densely streaked. Juvenile plumage is similar. The eyes are large and yellow. L: *c.* 16″, Wt: *c.* 14 oz.

Its wailing "crree-ee" can be heard, especially in the evening, repeated several times. Swelling "tleet" sequences are also uttered.

Distribution: Southeast England, west, south and southeast Europe, northeast Germany, Asia, North Africa, the Canaries. A partial migrant in Europe, it winters in the southwest and the Mediterranean area.
Habitat: Stony semi-deserts, Salicornia-steppes, dry heaths and chalk-downs, corn-fields where these last have been put under cultivation.

Breeding: Probably sexually mature at 2 years. Nest: a shallow scrape "lined" with small stones, rabbit droppings or straws. The normally 2 yellow-grey or pale brown, dark-marked eggs are brooded by ♂ and ♀ for around 25–27 days. The young become independent at about 6 weeks. Single- or double-brooded.
Food: Insects, worms, snails, sometimes small frogs, lizards and mice, occasionally small young birds.

Mediterranean Gull · *Larus melanocephalus* (p. 214) Above

Black-headed Gull · *Larus ridibundus* (p. 215) with young Below

Pratincole · *Glareola pratincola* (L.) (Illustration precedes p. 194, above)

Family: Pratincoles and coursers (Glareolidae)
Description: In breeding dress it is olive-brown above with white upper tail-coverts; the tail is deeply forked. The creamy throat is sharply demarcated from the buffish breast by a black line; this is absent in winter. Juvenile plumage resembles the winter adult's. The pratincole flies like a tern, is an agile runner, and raises and lowers its tail. L: *c.* 10″.

The bird has a tern-like "kirreh" call.

Distribution: Spain and south Portugal, the Camargue, the Po delta, Sicily, southeast Europe, Asia, Africa. It is a summer visitor to Europe, wintering chiefly in arid regions south of the Sahara.
Habitat: Steppe-country near water, mud-banks with low vegetation, fallow ground, flooded areas.

Breeding: Sexually mature at 1 year. A sparsely-lined scrape on the ground serves as a nest. ♂ and ♀ take turns incubating the eggs (usually 3, sandy with dark blotching) for about 3 weeks. Single-brooded.
Food: Insects, especially grasshoppers, locusts and flies.

Great Skua (Bonxie) · *Stercorarius skua* (Brünn.)
(Illustration precedes p. 194, below)

Family: Skuas (Stercorariidae)
Description: The upperparts are dark brown with paler streaks, the underparts earth-brown with some dark streaking on neck and breast. A white patch along the base of the primary feathers shows in flight. The central tail feathers extend slightly beyond the others. The legs and stout bill are blackish. Summer, winter and juvenile plumages are similar. L: *c.* 23″, Wt: *c.* 3½ lb.

Intruders near the nest are "dive-bombed". The Bonxie makes gruff "og-og-og" and "harr-harr" calls.

Distribution: Iceland, the Faeroes, Orkneys and Shetlands (rare elsewhere in N. Scotland), southern South America and the Antarctic. It

Black Tern · *Chlidonias niger* (p. 218) ▷

winters at sea, some European birds staying in southwest Continental waters, others ranging across the Atlantic.

Habitat: Moorland with short vegetation, sometimes grassy ground, near the coast. The open ocean and offshore waters outside the breeding season.

Breeding: It does not breed until several years old, and usually breeds in loose colonies. A shallow, sparsely grass-lined hollow forms the nest. The 2 eggs are olive-brown with dark spots or blotches. Incubation, by ♂ and ♀, lasts 4 weeks. Single-brooded.

Food: Fish, much of it "pirated" by harrying seabirds until they disgorge their catch; it also kills many adult and young birds of up to gull-size, and will eat carrion.

Allied species: The Arctic Skua (*S. parasiticus*) is smaller. The pointed central tail-feathers project well beyond the rest. Breeding range: Iceland, Spitzbergen, north Scotland (numerous only in the Shetlands and Orkneys), the coasts of Scandinavia, Greenland, arctic Asia and North America.

The Pomarine Skua (*S. pomarinus*) has long, twisted, spatulate central tail-feathers. It breeds in northeasternmost Europe, west Greenland, arctic Asia and North America.

The Long-tailed Skua (*S. longicaudus*) is smaller and more lightly built than the above species; its long central tail-feathers are pointed. It nests in north and northeast Europe, Greenland, arctic Asia and North America. In these 3 species some birds are dark all over, others are pale or even white below. Juveniles have somewhat barred plumage; their central tail-feathers scarcely project.

Great Black-backed Gull · *Larus marinus* L.
(Illustration follows p. 195, above)

Family: Gulls and terns (Laridae)
Description: Adults are white with black back and black, white-edged wings. The bill is yellow with a red spot on the lower mandible; the

Kittiwake · *Rissa tridactyla* (p. 218) Above

Whiskered Tern · *Chlidonias hybrida* (p. 219) Below

legs and feet are flesh-coloured. Immatures are buffish, heavily chequered with grey-brown above, off-white below with light streaking on neck and throat, and have dark bills. Adult plumage is gradually acquired over several years. L: *c.* 29", Wt: *c.* 4 lb.

A variety of deep calls is uttered, the commonest being a barking "owk-owk-owk".

Distribution: North and northwest Europe, France, Belgium, Greenland, North America. It is a partial migrant in Europe, wintering mainly on coasts.

Habitat: Seacoasts or their vicinity, islands—breeding on cliffs, moorland, tundra. It feeds by muddy and sandy shores, harbours and rubbish tips, and at sea (also following ships).

Breeding: Sexually mature at 4–5 years. Nest: a shallow structure of locally available material. ♂ and ♀ incubate the 2–3 brownish, dark-spotted eggs for about 26 days. The young become independent after about 7 weeks. Single-brooded.

Food: Fish, molluscs, worms, crustaceans, offal and scraps, small mammals, small seabirds and their eggs.

Allied species: The roughly similar-sized Glaucous Gull (*L. hyperboreus*) is white with pale grey back, white flight-feathers, yellow bill and eye-ring, flesh-coloured legs. It breeds in Iceland, Spitzbergen, islands in the Arctic Ocean, Greenland, arctic Asia and North America.

The herring gull-sized Iceland Gull (*L. glaucoides*) has similar plumage to the glaucous gull but has a red eye-ring in the breeding season. It nests in Greenland and Baffin Land (but not Iceland!). Small numbers of both species winter in northwest Europe.

Herring Gull · *Larus argentatus* Pontopp.
(Illustrations follow p. 195, below, and p. 215)

Family: Gulls and terns (Laridae)
Description: Adults are white with pale grey backs; their wing-tips are

Common Tern · *Stern hirundo* (p. 223) Above ▷

Arctic Tern · *Sterna paradisea* (p. 226) Below ▷

black with white spots, their bills yellow with a red spot on the lower mandible. Their legs are flesh-pink (yellow in certain races). The head is faintly streaked in winter. Immature plumage is much as in the great black-backed gull. L: 22″, Wt: *c*. 2½ lb.

Voice: sequences like "kiaow-kiaow-kiaowkiowkyowkyowkyow"; a gruff "gagaga". It has a wide repertory of variations.

Distribution: The coasts of Europe, islands in the North Atlantic; north and central Asia, northern North America. It winters around coasts and increasingly inland.

Habitat: It breeds on cliffs (and sometimes buildings), islands, and in places sand dunes or boggy moorland. It feeds by the shore, at sea, in fields and on dumps, and roosts in bays or on reservoirs.

Breeding and *Food:* Much as for great black-backed gull. Single-brooded.

Lesser Black-backed Gull · *Larus fuscus* L.
(Illustration precedes p. 198)

Family: Gulls and terns (Laridae)
Description: The adult is white with back and wings dark grey (almost black in Scandinavian birds), and has yellow legs. Juveniles are very like young herring gulls. L: *c*. 21″, Wt: *c*. 2¼ lb.

The calls resemble the herring gull's, and are between the latter and great black-back's in pitch.

Distribution: Iceland, the British Isles, Scandinavia, west European coasts, northwest Siberia. A partial migrant, many birds winter in West Africa but some stay in west and south Europe.

Habitat: Coasts, boggy moors, inland waters. It often occurs well out at sea.

Breeding and *Food:* As for herring gull, but it less often breeds on cliffs.

Allied species: Audouin's Gull (*L. audouini*), one of the rarest gulls, breeds locally in the Mediterranean area. It looks like the rather larger

Little Tern · *Sterna albifrons* (p. 227) Above

Gull-billed Tern · *Gelochelidon nilotica* (p. 219) Below

herring gull, but has a coral-red bill with a black band and yellow tip, while the legs are dark olive-green.

The roughly great black-backed-sized Great Black-headed Gull (*L. ichthyaëtus*) has a black head and white eye-rings in breeding plumage. Otherwise, and also in winter dress, it resembles the herring gull. It breeds by the Sea of Azov, the Caspian and in central Asia.

Common Gull · *Larus canus* L. (Illustration follows p. 199, above)

Family: Gulls and terns (Laridae)
Description: It is white with a light grey back. The wing-tips are black with white spots. The bill and legs are greenish-yellow. Juveniles are brown with dark markings above and have a white tail with a dark band near the tip. Their underparts are whitish with fine grey streaking on neck and breast. Their legs are flesh-coloured, their bills flesh or yellowish at the base, dark-tipped. L: *c.* 16", Wt: *c.* 12 oz.

The calls are higher and shriller than the herring gull's. They may be rendered "gehgeh" and "keeya".

Distribution: Iceland, the Faeroes, the British Isles, Holland, Denmark, north Germany, local inland in mid-Europe, northeast Europe, Siberia, the Caucasus, the Caspian Sea, northwest North America. It is a partial migrant in Europe, wintering coastally and inland.
Habitat: Coasts, lakes, moorland and hill-lochans. Farmland in winter.

Breeding: Sexually mature at 2–3 years. The nest, of dry plant material, is often on a rocky islet, sometimes among short vegetation. Incubation by ♂ and ♀ of the 3 olive-brown, dark-spotted eggs takes over 3 weeks. The young become independent at around 5 weeks. Single-brooded.
Food: Worms, shellfish, insects, fish, birds' eggs, small vertebrates, scraps.

Slender-billed Gull · *Larus genei* Brème
(Illustration follows p. 199, below)

Family: Gulls and terns (Laridae)
Description: It is white with a pale grey back. In flight the outer wing

Sandwich Tern · *Sterna sandvicensis* (p. 222) ▷

is white, narrowly edged black at the rear. Legs and bill are red. Juveniles have yellowish bill and legs and a black terminal bar on the tail. Their upperparts have grey-brown markings. L: 17".

The calls have a nasal sound, like "kraihng"; a hard "gack-gack..." is used too.

Distribution: South Spain, the Camargue, Sardinia, the Black and Caspian Seas, local in Asia. It is a partial migrant, wintering in the Mediterranean area and the Persian Gulf.
Habitat: Shallow brackish and fresh-water lakes in open flat country. Broad, more or less treeless river-deltas are favoured.

Breeding and *Food:* As for black-headed gull.

Mediterranean Gull · *Larus melanocephalus* Temm.
(Illustration precedes p. 202, above)

Family: Gulls and terns (Laridae)
Description: Summer plumage is white with a black head and white eye-ring. The primaries are whitish; bill and legs are red. Winter plumage: the head is white with grey streaking on crown and nape. Juvenile: the back is brown (lightly streaked), the primaries are blackish-brown, the tail has a dark terminal band. L: *c.* 15", Wt: *c.* 8 oz.

The bird's call sounds like "eh-aa", the "aa" having a nasal quality (Löhrl).

Distribution: Lower Austria, east Greece, the Aegean, the Black Sea, Asia Minor, the Gobi Desert. It winters around the Mediterranean. A rare wanderer to Britain.
Habitat: Fresh-water lakes with vegetated margins, flat river valleys, saltmarshes. Outside the breeding season it may occur by water of any kind.

Breeding and *Food:* Details similar to black-headed gull.

Allied species: The similar but much smaller Little Gull (*L. minutus*) has no white eye-ring; it has dark under-wings. It breeds in Holland, Denmark, south Sweden, the eastern Baltic, east Europe, locally by the Caspian and in Turkey.

Black-headed Gull · *Larus ridibundus* L. (Illustration p. 201, below)
Family: Gulls and terns (Laridae)
Description: Summer plumage is white with pale grey back and chocolate-brown head. The white eye-ring is inconspicuous. The winter plumage is similar except that the head is white with a dark spot behind the eye. Legs and bill are always red. Juveniles are a mottled brown above, white below and have a dark terminal tail-band. Their bills and legs are dusky yellowish. Old and young birds have little black on the primaries, and the leading edge of the wing is white. L: 15″, Wt: *c.* 9 oz.

Of the various calls, the most familiar is a shrieking "krrarr".

Distribution: Iceland, the Faeroes, the British Isles, south Scandinavia, mid- and east Europe, the Camargue, northeast Italy; also right across Asia. In Europe it is partially migrant, wintering in the centre, west and around the Mediterranean.

Habitat: Coastal dunes, islands, saltings, inland lakes, marshes and moors. It feeds by the coast and in fields. Outside the breeding season birds even frequent park-lakes in cities, readily taking the food people throw for them. Like other gulls, this species breeds in colonies. In winter large numbers roost together in bays and on reservoirs.

Breeding: Sexually mature at 2–3 years. Nests vary from sparsely-lined scrapes on shingle to well-built ones on grass or on floating marsh-vegetation. The 2–3 brownish, olive or greenish, dark-spotted eggs are incubated by ♂ and ♀ for 22–24 days. The young leave the nest at 2–3 days, but remain in the proximity until able to fly when about 6 weeks old. Single-brooded.

Food: Chiefly worms, insects, fish, scraps.

Allied species: Sabine's Gull (*Xema sabini*) in breeding plumage has a slate-grey head; this becomes whitish with grey streaking at the rear in winter. There is a thin black "collar". The outer primaries are black, the inner ones and the secondaries white; the tail is forked. It breeds on Spitzbergen, in north Greenland, arctic Asia and North America.

The white Ivory Gull (*Pagophila eburnea*) has black legs and a yellow, black-tipped bill. Breeding sites: Spitzbergen, Nova Zemlaya, islands in the Arctic Ocean, north Greenland, arctic North America.

Guillemot · *Uria aalge* (p. 227) (Left: Herring Gull) ▷

Kittiwake · *Rissa tridactyla* (L.) (Illustration precedes p. 206, above)

Family: Gulls and terns (Laridae)
Description: This gull is white with a light grey back (the back of the head also goes greyish in winter). The wing-tips are black without white spots. Juveniles have a black band across the back of the neck and a dark bar along the inner wing which, with the black outer primaries, gives a zig-zag effect in flight. L: *c.* 16″, Wt: *c.* 15 oz.

Voice: calls at breeding cliffs include "kittiwaak" and "gehgehgeh".

Distribution: North and northwest Europe, the west coast of France, islands in the Arctic Ocean, northeast Asia, Greenland, Newfoundland, Baffin Land, West Alaska, the Aleutians. It is a partial migrant, wintering out in the Atlantic and in European waters.
Habitat: Rocky coasts, locally also breeding on dockside buildings. It feeds at sea and is rarely seen inland, unless storm-driven.

Breeding: Birds do not breed until several years old. Colonies are generally on steep cliffs or stacks with the nests of seaweed and grass on narrow ledges. ♂ and ♀ incubate the 2–3 pale brown, dark-blotched eggs for rather over 3 weeks. The young do not wander from the nest—an instinct important for survival on cliffs. They can fly when 5–6 weeks old. Single-brooded.
Food: Fish, crustaceans, molluscs, sometimes insects and scraps.

Black Tern · *Chlidonias niger* (L.) (Illustration follows p. 203)

Family: Gulls and terns (Laridae)
Description: Breeding plumage is almost entirely blackish-grey with white under wing-coverts. The tail is forked. Winter adults, and juveniles, are mainly greyish above, white below and have a dark mark in front of each wing. L: 9½″, Wt: *c.* 2½ oz.

The calls may be rendered "krek-krek" and "kriaah".

Distribution: Mid-, east and south Europe, south Scandinavia; local in the Po valley and Sardinia; also in Asia and North America. A summer visitor to Europe, it winters in tropical Africa. Migrants quite often pass through England.
Habitat: Shallow lakes and pools with an abundance of water plants, swampy areas with patches of open water, marshy river-deltas.

218

Breeding: Perhaps sexually mature at 2 years. The nest, of plant matter, is placed on floating debris or a mat of water plants. Incubation by both partners of the generally 2–3 olive, dark-spotted eggs takes barely 3 weeks. The young begin to fly when about 3 weeks old. Single-brooded.

Food: Insects, worms, small fish, tadpoles and frogs.

Allied species: The similar White-winged Black Tern (*C. leucopterus*) differs in summer by having white upper wing-coverts and tail. The bill and legs are red in summer. Winter plumage is much like the last species but lacks the black marks in the "shoulder" region. It breeds in the Po valley, southeast and east Europe, locally in Asia and east Africa. Birds occasionally wander as far as Britain when on passage.

Whiskered Tern · *Chlidonias hybrida* (Pall.)
(Illustration precedes p. 206, below)

Family: Gulls and terns (Laridae)

Description: Breeding plumage: grey with blackish belly, black crown, white cheeks and sides of neck. The tail is slightly forked, the bill and tail are red. Winter plumage: underparts white, upperparts pale grey with the crown and nape darker, the forehead white. Juveniles are like winter adults but have mottled upperparts. L: *c.* 10″, Wt: *c.* 3 oz.

The calls are a rasping "skreeah" or a hard "ket-ket".

Distribution: Local in west and central France, the Camargue, Iberia, the Po delta, southeast Europe, Asia, Australia, New Zealand, Africa, Madagascar. European birds are summer visitors which winter in tropical Africa.

Habitat: Lakes and pools with marshy margins, marshy river-deltas, etc.

Breeding and *Food:* Much as in the black tern; the usually 3 eggs are paler and less heavily spotted than in that species.

Gull-billed Tern · *Gelochelidon nilotica* (Gmel.)
(Illustration precedes p. 210, below)

Family: Gulls and terns (Laridae)

Description: Breeding plumage: white with black crown and bill, grey

Razorbill · *Alca torda* (p. 230) ▷

upperparts. The tail is forked. Winter plumage: the head is white with the nape region grey and a broad black stripe from the eye to the ear-region. Juveniles are also like this, but mottled above. L: *c.* 15″, Wt: *c.* 7 oz.

The call is a rapidly uttered "hagagaga", having a laughing quality.

Distribution: Local in south and southeast Europe, on the Atlantic coast of France and Holland, in Denmark, Asia, Australia, South, Central and North America. It is a summer visitor to Europe and winters in tropical Africa.

Habitat: Brackish and saline lagoons, also inland waters; low sandy islands, broad river-deltas.

Breeding: Sexually mature at 2–3 years. The nest is on the ground among short grass or quite exposed: a slight depression lined with a few grasses. The mostly 3 pale brownish, dark-spotted eggs are incubated by ♂ and ♀ for 22–23 days. The young are able to fly after 4–5 weeks. Single-brooded.

Food: Mainly insects, worms, small vertebrates.

Allied species: The Caspian Tern (*Hydroprogne caspia*) is almost herring gull-sized and in summer plumage may be told by its bright red bill and black crown, which becomes streaked blackish and white in winter. It breeds locally on the east and west coasts of, and islands in, the Baltic, by the Black and Caspian Seas, in Asia, Africa, Australia, New Zealand and North America.

Sandwich Tern · *Sterna sandvicensis* Lath. (Illustration follows p. 211)

Family: Gulls and terns (Laridae)
Description: ♂ and ♀ are white with light grey back and wings. The black crown has a slight shaggy crest at the rear. The bill is black and yellow-tipped; the legs are black. Winter plumage is similar apart from

Puffin · *Fratercula arctica* (p. 231) Above

Pin-tailed Sandgrouse · *Pterocles alchata* (p. 234) Below

the white forehead. In juveniles the back is mottled, the crown looks brownish. L: *c.* 16″, Wt: *c.* 9 oz.

Voice: a hoarse "kirrik"; also rasping and guttural calls.

Distribution: Coasts of the British Isles (in Hampshire and from Suffolk northwards), west Europe from France to south Sweden; local in the Camargue and by the Black Sea; also by the Caspian, in Tunisia, Central and southern North America, local in South America. It is a summer visitor in Europe, wintering chiefly along the coast of west Africa.

Habitat: Flat sandy or shingly shores with scanty vegetation.

Breeding: Sexually mature at 4–5 years. Like other terns, it nests in colonies. During ground display the partners circle round each other with drooped wings and erected crests (see plate). Nest-hollows are "moulded" in sand or shingle, sometimes in the lee of a marram grass clump. Usually 1–2 eggs, creamy or sandy with dark brown spots, are laid. Incubation by ♂ and ♀ takes 22–24 days. The young become free-flying and independent at around 5 weeks. Single-brooded.

Food: All taken at sea: small fish, marine worms and molluscs.

Allied species: The Roseate Tern (*S. dougalli*) resembles common and arctic terns but has a largely black bill in summer, longer tail streamers, and distinctive calls (rasping "aaak", soft "chu-ick"). It breeds very locally on the coasts of the British Isles, in the Camargue, on the Azores and Madeira, locally in north and east Africa, in southeast Asia, Australia, southern North and Central America.

Common Tern · *Sterna hirundo* L. (Illustration follows p. 207, above)

Family: Gulls and terns (Laridae)

Description: Breeding dress is white, pale grey above with a black cap. The tail is markedly forked. The red bill has a black tip, the legs are red. Winter plumage: forehead white, bill mainly black. Juveniles are like winter adults with mottled brown backs. L: *c.* 14″, Wt: *c.* 6 oz.

The screeching "*kee*arr" call denotes alarm, but it is also used on migration; a hard "ki-kit-kit-kirrr" is a contact note.

Distribution: The British Isles, Faeroes, coastal and southern Scandinavia,

Stock Dove · *Columba oenas* (p. 235) ▷

most of continental Europe except Italy and inland Iberia; large areas of Asia, west Africa, the Azores, Canaries and Madeira, North and Central America. A summer visitor to Europe, it winters largely along the west African coast.

Habitat: Coastal dunes, shingle, salt-marshes and islands, inland waters with vegetated shallows, shingle banks or islets.

Breeding: It does not usually breed until 3 years old. The nest-scrape is on sand, shingle or short grass, or on a mat of floating water-plants. ♂ and ♀ brood the 2–3 greenish or olive-brown, darkly blotched eggs for about 3 weeks. The young become able to fly at 3–4 weeks. Single-brooded.

Food: Fish, water-insects, molluscs, crustaceans, worms.

Arctic Tern · *Sterna paradisea* Pontopp. (formerly *S. macrura*)
(Illustration follows p. 207, below)

Family: Gulls and terns (Laridae)
Description: Breeding plumage resembles the common tern's but the breast is tinged grey and the bill is all red. Adults in winter and juveniles are very like common terns, although the tail-streamers extend a little beyond the folded wings, and the legs are very short. L: *c.* 16″, Wt: *c.* 4 oz.

The most often heard call is "kee*arr*"—with the second syllable emphasised.

Distribution: Iceland, the Faeroes, most coasts of the British Isles and northwest Europe (south to Brittany), Scandinavia, northeast Europe, Spitzbergen, northern Asia and islands in the Arctic Ocean, the Greenland coast, northern North America. A summer visitor, it winters on the south African coast and in the Antarctic Ocean.

Habitat: Flat and low rocky shores and off-shore islands, in the north also moorland and marshes inland. Migrants sometimes visit inland waters.

Breeding and *Food:* Similar to common tern; the clutch is 1–3.

Collared Dove · *Streptopelia decaocto* (p. 238)

226

Little Tern · *Sterna albifrons* Pall. (Illustration precedes p. 210, above)
Family: Gulls and terns (Laridae)
Description: Breeding plumage: white, pale grey above, with the white forehead sharply demarcated from the black cap and a black stripe from bill to eye. The bill is yellow, tipped black; the legs are yellow. Winter plumage: the white forehead merges into the grey of the crown. Juveniles resemble winter adults but have dark markings on the back. L: *c.* 9″, Wt: *c.* 1¾ oz.

Frequently heard calls are a sharp "kitt-kitt…", a chattering "kirri-kiki-kirri-kirri" and a harsh "krreeik".
Distribution: The coast of nearly all Europe (including the British Isles) but only sporadic in Scandinavia; locally inland. Asia, the coasts of Australia, Africa and Central and southern North America. A summer visitor to Europe, it winters chiefly along coastal reaches of west Africa.
Habitat: Shingly and sandy beaches and dunes, areas of sparse vegetation by brackish pools and saline lagoons, etc.
Breeding: Generally sexually mature at 2 years. Colonies tend to be small. During courtship the ♂ presents small fish to the ♀. Nest-scrapes are lined with the shingle or pebbles around. Incubation of the 2–3 eggs is by ♂ and ♀ and takes 20–22 days. The well-camouflaged chicks leave the nest soon after hatching and hide by crouching flat. They begin to fly at 3 weeks. Single-brooded.
Food: Tiny fish, crustaceans, worms and insects.

Guillemot · *Uria aalge* (Pontopp.) (Illustration follows p. 215)
Family: Auks (Alcidae)
Description: In summer the upperparts, throat and neck are blackish-brown, the underparts white. Some birds have a white eye-ring, extending back as a thin stripe to the ear ("bridled guillemots"). In winter the throat and cheeks are white with a black line running back from the eye. Juveniles are similar. L: *c.* 16½″, Wt: *c.* 2¼ lb.

Voice: a harsh, growling "arrr" and "errr".

Wood Pigeon · *Columba palumbus* (p. 235) Above ▷

Turtle Dove · *Streptopelia turtur* (p. 239) Below ▷

Distribution: Suitable coasts of Iceland, the Faeroes, British Isles, west Europe south to Spain; Heligoland, locally in the Baltic; east Asia, northern North America and east Greenland. It is a partial migrant, wintering along the coasts of west and south Europe.

Habitat: Steep sea-cliffs and the flat tops of isolated stacks. Outside the breeding season it largely frequents offshore waters.

Breeding: Sexually mature at 2–3 years. It breeds in colonies with birds often very close together along the ledges. The single pear-shaped egg may be bluish, greenish, whitish or reddish, blotched or covered with darker or black squiggles; it is laid on the bare rock. Incubation, by ♂ and ♀, takes *c.* 36 days (occasionally much longer). Both partners feed the chick. When only 2–3 weeks old it flutters down to the sea, where the parents continue to tend it. Single-brooded.

Food: Mainly small sea-fish, also crustaceans caught underwater.

Allied species: The similar Brünnich's Guillemot (*U. lomvia*) has a distinctly thicker bill with a pale line along the edges of the upper mandible; in winter it has no black line behind the eye. It breeds on the coasts of Iceland, Spitzbergen, various islands in the north Atlantic and Arctic Oceans, Greenland, northern North America, northeast Asia.

   The Black Guillemot or Tystie (*Cepphus grylle*) is smaller and in summer is all black with white wing-patches and red feet. Birds in winter dress appear off-white with blackish barring on the back. It breeds on the coasts of Ireland, west and north Scotland, Scandinavia, islands in the north Atlantic and the Arctic Ocean, Greenland, northern North America and north Asia. 1–2 rather pale eggs are laid in holes in cliffs or under boulders by the shore.

Razorbill · *Alca torda* L. (Illustration follows p. 219)

Family: Auks (Alcidae)

Description: The upperparts, head and neck are blackish, the underparts white. The bill, deep and laterally flattened, is black with a white vertical line on each side. A white line runs from the base of the bill to the eye. This is lacking in winter, when the front and sides of the neck become white. Juveniles are like winter adults but have less deep bills. L: *c.* 16″, Wt: *c.* 28 oz. Voice: a deep growling "karrr".

Cuckoo · *Cululus canorus* (p. 239)

Distribution: Coasts of the British Isles (except the southeast), western-most France, Fenno-Scandinavia, islands in the north Atlantic; Green-land, northeast North America. It is a resident and partial migrant in Europe, wintering off the coasts of west and southwest Europe.

Habitat: Sea-cliffs and steep rocky stacks. Outside the breeding season it lives mainly in offshore waters.

Breeding: Birds may first breed at 2 years. Razorbills breed in looser colonies than guillemots, with which they often associate. Egg colour varies from white to light brownish, with dark spots or blotches. Only one is laid, in a crevice or on a sheltered ledge of a cliff. ♂ and ♀ incubate for 33–39 days. They both feed the chick at the nest site for 2–3 weeks, at which stage it leaps to the sea to continue its growth, being still tended by at least one parent. Single-brooded.

Food: Small fish, crustaceans, molluscs and marine worms, caught by diving from the surface.

Allied species: The Little Auk (*Plautus alle*), of plump starling-size, is mainly black above, white below, the dark brown neck and throat turning white in winter. It breeds on sea-cliffs above the Arctic Circle in the Atlantic, Arctic Ocean and Greenland. Numbers are occasionally storm-blown inland.

Puffin · *Fratercula arctica* (L.) (Illustration precedes p. 222, above)
Family: Auks (Alcidae)

Description: Breeding plumage is black above, white below; the sides of the face are grey-white. The laterally flattened, very deep bill has zones of grey-blue, yellow and red; the legs are red. Winter dress: the bill is less deep and bright, the legs are yellow. Juveniles have dark, still thinner bills and flesh-coloured legs. L: *c.* 12″, Wt: *c.* 14 oz.

The gruff calls may be rendered "orrr" or "rro".

Distribution: Coasts of the British Isles (not the southeast), west and north Scandinavia, islands of the north Atlantic, Greenland, northeast North America. European birds are partial migrants, wintering off western and southern Europe.

Habitat: Rocky islands and coasts with grassy slopes and cliffs. It keeps mainly to offshore waters outside the breeding season.

Barn Owl · *Tyto alba* (p. 242) ▷

Breeding: Puffins nest colonially, using bills and feet to excavate burrows up to 7 ft. long in turf; natural cavities among rocks are also used at times. The single egg, whitish with faint darker markings, is laid on the floor at the end of the hole and incubated chiefly by the ♀ for 40–43 days. Both parents feed the chick in the burrow for 6 weeks, then abandon it; after fasting a few days it flutters down to the sea by night and learns to fish on its own. Single-brooded.

Food: Small fish, crustaceans, marine molluscs and worms.

Pin-tailed Sandgrouse · *Pterocles alchata* (L.) (Illustration p. 221)

Family: Sandgrouse (Pteroclididae)

Description: The upperparts are light brown and yellow with dark wave-like barring. The chin is black in the ♂, paler in the ♀; the belly is white. At rest the needle-like centre tail-feathers extend far beyond the wing-tips. In flight the largely white underside, long tail-feathers, and dark grey flight-feathers are conspicuous. L: *c.* 12½".

Calls sounding like "katarr-katarr" are uttered in flight.

Distribution: The Iberian peninsula, the "Crau" in southern France, north Africa and southwest Asia. It is predominantly resident.

Habitat: Scantily vegetated steppes, semi-deserts.

Breeding: Sexually mature at 1 year. Nest: a shallow unlined scrape. Incubation of the 2–3 pale brown, dark-spotted eggs is by ♂ and ♀, taking around 4 weeks. The young are nidifugous and are fed by ♂ and ♀ from their crops. Single- or double-brooded.

Food: Seeds and green plant matter growing in the above habitats.

Allied species: The similar Black-bellied Sandgrouse (*P. orientalis*) differs in having a black belly and black flight-feathers. It breeds in the Iberian peninsula, north Africa and southwest Asia.

Pallas's Sandgrouse (*Syrrhaptes paradoxus*) has pale under-wings and a dark belly-patch. It is found over the Asiatic steppes; numbers occasionally wandered to western Europe in the past.

Stock Dove · *Columba oenas* L. (Illustration follows p. 223)

Family: Pigeons and doves (Columbidae)

Description: ♂ and ♀ are mainly bluish-grey with a vinous tinge on the breast and blackish tip to the tail. Note the absence of white on both wings and rump. The sides of the neck have a greenish gloss. Juveniles are similar. L: *c.* 13", Wt: 9–10¾ oz.

The song is a hollow-sounding "hoowoop-hoowoop…".

Distribution: Almost all of Europe except the extreme north and northeast; west and central Asia, north Africa. It is a partial migrant in Europe, wintering in the west and south. (British birds are resident.)
Habitat: Woods with mature trees, large parks and farmland with old hollow trees, inland and coastal cliffs.

Breeding: Sexually mature at 2 years. Nests may be in holes in trees (or nestboxes), among rocks, rabbit holes in sand-banks, etc. Nest material —twigs and straws—is often very scanty. The generally 2 pure white eggs are brooded by both partners, hatching after 16–18 days; the young fly when about 4 weeks old. 2–3 (even up to 5) broods are reared in a year.
Food: Weed seeds, corn, tree seeds, berries and snails.

Allied species: The Rock Dove (*C. livia*), ancestor of the domestic pigeon, has a whitish rump. It breeds in sea-caves and cliff-holes (also inland in southern countries), on the Faeroes, the coasts of Britain and west France, southwest and southern Europe; Asia, Africa, the Canaries, Azores, Madeira and Cape Verde Isles. Over much of Britain and elsewhere many colonies have a large admixture of escaped homing pigeons and their descendants.

Wood Pigeon · *Columba palumbus* L. (Illustration follows p. 227, above)

Family: Pigeons and doves (Columbidae)
Description: This is the largest pigeon species. It is blue-grey above with a white patch on each side of the neck (lacking in otherwise similar juveniles) and a white band across each wing. The tail is quite long with a broad black terminal band. The breast is vinous, the belly whitish-grey. L: *c.* 16", Wt: *c.* 18 oz.

The well-known song of the ♂ goes "coo*croo*ocroo-coocoo-coocoo…".

Eagle Owl · *Bubo bubo* (p. 243) ▷

Distribution: Europe except for Iceland and the extreme north and northeast; north Africa, the Azores, Madeira. A partial migrant in Europe, it winters mainly in the west and the Mediterranean area, often feeding in big flocks.

Habitat: Woods of all kinds up to the tree-limit, farmland and orchards, parks and even some city centres.

Breeding: Sexually mature at 1 year. The flat nests of twigs are in trees, tall bushes or hedges, and occasionally on buildings. ♂ and ♀ incubate the normally 2 white eggs for 15½–18 days. The fledging period varies from 3–4 weeks. Double- or treble-brooded.

Food: Seeds of plants and trees, berries, plant-leaves (especially clover), a few worms, snails and insect larvae. The large amounts of grain and green vegetable crops it eats make it a serious pest on farmland.

Collared Dove · *Streptopelia decaocto* (Frivaldszky)
(Illustration precedes p. 226)

Family: Pigeons and doves (Columbidae)

Description: It is uniformly light grey-brown above, light grey below with a soft pink flush on the breast. There is a black half-collar round the nape (lacking in juveniles). The primaries are blackish. L: *c.* 11″, Wt: *c.* 7 oz.

Song: a resonant "coo*coo*coo coo*coo*coo..."; hoarse mewing notes are also uttered.

Distribution: The species has spread from southwest Asia across central and much of western Europe and south Scandinavia this century. It first bred in England in 1954 and is now found all over the British Isles. It also breeds in Asia and Africa. Resident.

Habitat: In Europe almost always around habitations.

Breeding: It breeds when 1 year old. ♂♂ often display on television aerials and chimneys. The twig nests are in trees (often evergreens), tall shrubs, and ledges on buildings. Incubation of the normally 2 white eggs is by ♂ and ♀, taking 16–17 days. The young fly when barely 3 weeks old. There are 3 broods annually, sometimes more.

Food: Seeds, poultry food, berries, snails, kitchen scraps.

Long-eared Owl · *Asio otus* (p. 246)

Turtle Dove · *Streptopelia turtur* (L.)
(Illustration follows p. 227, below)

Family: Pigeons and doves (Columbidae)
Description: The crown and nape are grey; on each side of the neck is a white patch with 3 horizontal black stripes. The back is warm brown with black flecking. The throat and breast have a vinous flush, the remaining underparts are largely white. The tail is black with narrow white edging. Juveniles lack the neck-markings. L: *c.* 11″, Wt: *c.* 6 oz.

Song: a purring "trurr-turrturr-trurr-trurr…".

Distribution: Most of England and Wales, mainland Europe except Scandinavia and the northeast; Asia, local in north Africa. It is a summer visitor to Europe, wintering mostly in tropical Africa.
Habitat: Open mixed and deciduous woods with a good shrub-layer, plantations, overgrown field-hedges, bushy commons.
Breeding: The general pattern is like that of other doves. The small, flimsy twig nest is built in a bush, often thorny, or small tree. 2 white eggs make the usual clutch; incubation takes 13–15 days. Single- or double-brooded.
Food: Chiefly weed seeds.

Cuckoo · *Cuculus canorus* L. (Illustration precedes p. 230)

Family: Cuckoos (Cuculidae)
Description: The upperparts, neck and throat are bluish-grey, the breast and belly whitish with grey barring. All ♂♂ are of this colour, but occasional ♀♀ show reddish-brown instead of grey colouring. Juveniles are grey-brown above, completely barred below. It is rather hawk-like in flight. L: 13″, Wt: *c.* 3½ oz.

The "song" of the ♂ is "cuc-coo" with the 2nd syllable falling. This becomes trisyllabic in excitement. A guttural "gwagagag" may also be heard (hence the name "Gowk"). The ♀ makes a bubbling "kwickwick-wick…". Fledglings utter a persistent "zeers…".

Distribution: Europe, except the extreme northeast and islands in the north Atlantic. Also over most of Asia, much of Africa. A summer visitor in Europe, it winters in tropical and southern Africa.

Scops Owl · *Otus scops* (p. 247) ▷

Habitat: Woodland of all kinds, farmland, reedbeds, moorland.

Breeding: Cuckoos breed when 1 year old and are brood-parasites; they are promiscuous and do not live in pairs. A fertilised ♀ lays 1 egg in perhaps 10–15 nests of small birds. In some areas the eggs closely resemble those of the usual host-species. The young cuckoo hatches after 12½ days and pushes other nestlings or eggs over the nest-rim. It leaves the nest at about 3 weeks but the foster-parents continue feeding it for 3 more weeks.

Food: Insects and their larvae, especially hairy caterpillars, whose hairs stick and form a furry lining to the mucous membrane of the stomach. From time to time this is cast off and brought up like a pellet. Spiders and worms are eaten too.

Allied species: The Oriental Cuckoo (*C. orientalis*) occurs in northeast Europe, as well as across Siberia and east Asia.

The Great Spotted Cuckoo (*Clamator glandarius*) is grey-brown with white flecking above; it has a grey crest at the rear of the head, and is cream-coloured below. It parasitises magpies and other Corvidae. It breeds in the Mediterranean area, Asia Minor and locally in Africa.

Barn Owl · *Tyto alba* (Scop.) (Illustration follows p. 231)

Family: Barn owls (Tytonidae)

Description: ♂ and ♀ are pale golden-buff above, "dusted" with grey. The underparts are white or (as in north and east Europe) warm buff with more or less dark speckling. The eyes are black. Juveniles are similar. L: 13½″, Wt: *c.* 11 oz.

Voice: an eerie shriek, a snoring "chrrreeh". The young hiss.

Distribution: Europe, except for almost all Scandinavia, the northeast and southern Greece; almost all Africa, Arabia, India, various islands of the East Indies, Australia and Tasmania, North and South America. Predominantly resident.

Habitat: Open country with ruins and barns, belfries, fields or parkland with hollow trees, sometimes cliffs with caves and crevices.

Tawny Owl · *Strix aluco* (p. 247)

Breeding: The ♂ indicates the nest-hole or ledge to the ♀ by flying to it and snoring. Usually 4–7 white, rather rounded eggs are laid in a dark nook on the bare floor. Only the ♀ incubates, being fed during the 30–34 days of incubation by the ♂. The young stay in the nest-site for 9 weeks or more. There is 1 brood annually, 2 if rodents are especially plentiful.

Food: Mice and voles, shrews, moles, rats, large insects, sometimes also bats, weasels, small birds, reptiles and amphibians.

Eagle Owl · *Bubo bubo* (L.) (Illustration follows p. 235)

Family: Typical owls (Strigidae)

Description: The plumage is tawny with blackish streaking and mottling. On the head are 2 erectile feather-tufts or "ears". The iris is orange. Juveniles resemble adults, but their heads look woollier and have only slight ear-tufts. L: *c.* 28″, Wt: *c.* 4½ lb, ♀♀ usually heavier than ♂♂.

The "song" of the ♂ is a deep, falling "whoohu". The ♀ produces a higher pitched "hoohooo" or "hooo". During display gurgling and chuckling notes may also be heard. The young make hoarse, snoring hunger-calls.

Distribution: Europe with the exceptions of the extreme north and northeast, the British Isles, Iceland and much of the west. It is threatened with extinction in some regions where it does now occur. Further afield it is found in most of Asia and in north Africa. A resident.

Habitat: Mostly rocky country with ravines, extensive woodland. Here and there it occurs near habitations.

Breeding: It usually first breeds when 2–3 years old, and pairs for life. The nest site may be a fissure or hole in a cliff, a scrape on the ground, an old hawk's nest, etc. In spring both partners "sing" alternately. No nest-material is used. Incubation of the 1–3 white eggs takes about 35 days; it is all done by the ♀, the ♂ bringing food. The young leave the nest-site at 5–6 weeks and can fly at 8 weeks. Single-brooded.

Food: Chiefly mice, rats, rabbits, squirrels, dormice, hedgehogs, crows,

Little Owl · *Athene noctua* (p. 248) Above ▷

Pygmy Owl · *Glaucidium passerinum* (p. 249) Below ▷

pigeons, moorhens, and coots, sometimes even roe deer. Also large insects, frogs, lizards, fish, etc.

Long-eared Owl · *Asio otus* (L.) (Illustration preceding p. 238)

Family: Owls (Strigidae)
Description: ♂ and ♀ are buffish-brown with dark mottling and streaking, in addition to which the back and wings are tinged grey. The long "ears" are tufts of feathers. The iris is orange-red. L: 14″, Wt: *c.* 11 oz.

The display-call of the ♂ is a dull "hoob", repeated every 2–3 seconds. The ♀ answers this "song" with a similar but higher-pitched, vibrating call. Wing-clapping flights are made in early spring. At the nest a subdued "wegwegweg" is sometimes heard. The food-begging "feee" note of young birds sounds like an un-oiled gate.

Distribution: Europe, except for the extreme north and north-east; large stretches of Asia, North Africa and large parts of North America. In Europe it is a partial migrant with wintering areas in the centre, west and south.
Habitat: Woods with clearings, parkland. In Britain copses and coniferous tree-belts are often favoured.

Breeding: ♂ and ♀ call alternately on calm nights in March and April. Old nests of crows, magpies, birds of prey and woodpigeons are used for nesting. The 3–7 white, bluntly oval eggs are incubated by the ♀ alone, the ♂ bringing food. They hatch in 27–28 days. When about 24 days old the young leave the nest, after which they remain in their parents' care and are fed for a further 3 months or so. Normally single-brooded.
Food: Principally mice and shrews, more rarely small birds flushed from their roosts. Sometimes also beetles and frogs.

Allied species: The Short-eared Owl (*Asio flammeus*) has very short feather-tufts on the head, and bright yellow eyes. It is found across Eurasia above 40°N, also in North and South America. It is a bird of open country and nests on the ground.

Tengmalm's Owl · *Aegolius funereus* (p. 250)

Scops Owl · *Otus scops* (L.) (Illustration follows p. 239)

Family: Owls (Strigidae)
Description: The plumage is grey-brown with darker bark-like pattern-ing. The small ear-tufts can be raised or flattened. The iris is yellow. Juveniles are similar. L: 7½″, Wt: *c.* 3½ oz.

The "song" of the ♂ is a monotonous "kiew" repeated every 2-3 seconds, a characteristic feature of spring nights in southern Europe. The ♀ has a similar but higher and usually hoarser call. The young make soft "chew" and harsh "tcht" hunger calls ("ch" as in loch).

Distribution: Southern Europe as far as roughly 47°N, large areas of Asia and Africa. It winters mainly south of the Sahara.
Habitat: Open country with tree-clumps or scattered trees, avenues, old buildings, rocky areas with ravines.

Breeding: ♂ and ♀ call alternately on spring nights. The ♂ indicates the nest-site by flying to it and calling: a hole in a tree, wall, crag or earth bank, or sometimes an old magpie nest. The 3–6 roundish white eggs are incubated by the ♀ alone for some 26 days. During this period the ♂ feeds her. The owlets fly at about 4 weeks. Single-brooded.
Food: Mainly large insects, also mice and small birds.

Tawny Owl · *Strix aluco* L. (Illustration precedes p. 242)

Family: Owls (Strigidae)
Description: Two colour-phases occur: basically tawny-brown, and grey-ish. The back and breast are heavily streaked and finely barred. There are white spots in the shoulder-region. The eyes are blackish-brown. Juveniles are similar, more strongly barred. L: *c.* 15″, Wt: ♂ 14–18 oz, ♀ mostly over 18 oz.

The best-known call is a shrill "ke-wick". The hooting "song" of the ♂ goes "hooo-hoo-hooooooooooo", the final "phrase" having a quaver-ing quality. During display both partners make gurgling noises with a "u" or "ee" sound. The hunger-call of young birds is like "tissick".

Distribution: This is the commonest European owl, absent only from the northeast, north Scandinavia, Ireland and Iceland. It also breeds in north Africa and parts of Asia. It is a resident.

Habitat: Open woodland and parkland, large gardens, well-timbered farmland, rocky country, villages and towns. In Britain and parts of the Continent it has taken to breeding in city parks and buildings.

Breeding: Birds are sexually mature at 1 year, but some do not breed at all in years of vole scarcity. Sites include large holes in trees (or buildings), old nests of crows or hawks, old badger-setts, large crotches of trees or in hollows (at times formed by the bird) among roots of standing or fallen trees. From 1–6 rounded white eggs are laid (usually 2–3 in Britain). Incubation is by the ♀, fed by the ♂, and takes 28–29 days. The owlets leave the nest at 4–5 weeks, when still very weak on the wing. They are dependent on the parents for food for a further 2–3 months.

Food: Mostly small mammals up to rat-size; small birds, insects, etc.

Allied species: The Great Grey Owl (*S. nebulosa*) occurs in northern Europe and Siberia and in northwest North America. It is almost as big as the eagle owl. The deep "song" sounds like "hu-hu-huhuhuhu", gradually speeding up and rising in pitch.

The Ural Owl (*S. uralensis*), like a large, long-tailed tawny owl, is found in Lapland, northeast and southeast Europe as well as in Asia. Its "song" is a barking "huhu-hu-hu".

Little Owl · *Athene noctua* (Scop.) (Illustration follows p. 243, above)

Family: Owls (Strigidae)

Description: It is dark brown above with numerous large and small whitish spots; below it is greyish-white with dark brown streaks. The eyes are sulphur-yellow. Juvenile plumage is similar. L: 8½″, Wt: *c.* 6 oz.

The song of the ♂ is a rising, often repeated, querulous-sounding "oohg". During courtship this note tends to change to a frequently repeated mewing "kwiow". A shrill "kwiff-kwiff-kwiff" may also be heard. The young have a wheezing "tshsh" hunger-call.

Distribution: Europe except the northeast, Scandinavia, Iceland, Ireland and Scotland, although it is beginning to reach the latter from England, where it was introduced last century. Resident.

Habitat: Open country, e.g. farmland, parkland and waste land with scattered trees and small copses, old orchards, quarries, rock-gullies, ruins, barns and haystacks.

Breeding: Sexually mature at 1 year. Holes in trees and walls, rabbit-burrows, rock-crevices or crannies in buildings serve as nest-sites. The 3–7 white eggs are laid on the floor of the cavity and incubated for 28 days by the ♀, to whom the ♂ brings food. The young fly after about 4–5 weeks. Single-brooded.
Food: Small mammals to the size of moles, many insects, worms, birds to the size of a thrush.

Pygmy Owl · *Glaucidium passerinum* (L.) (Illustration follows p. 243, below)

Family: Owls (Strigidae)
Description: The upperparts are dark brown with whitish flecking; 4 pale bands run across the tail. The greyish-white underside has fine dark streaking. The iris is yellow. Juveniles are dark grey-brown above, streaked below. When excited the tail is raised and jerked backwards and forwards. L: *c.* 6½″, Wt: ♂ *c.* 2¼ oz, ♀ *c.* 2¾ oz.

Song of ♂: a monotonous "dee dee ..." or "dee-deedeedee dee-deedeedee...". The ♀ utters a sharp, rising "sseeht"; she goes "kiew-gewgewgewgewg" to invite the ♂ to mate with her. ♂ and ♀ give similar calls against intruders. Chiefly outside the breeding season a series of "dee" calls going up the scale may be heard from ♂ and ♀; these seem to be contact calls, rather than a sort of autumn song.

Distribution: The Alps, mountain ranges of central and east Europe, Scandinavia, Asia, western North America. It is mostly resident.
Habitat: Extensive mixed and coniferous woods, at high altitudes in the south, also on low ground in the north.

Breeding: The ♂ sings especially in the half-light of dawn and dusk in spring, but also in autumn. Woodpecker holes very often serve as nest-sites. The ♂ indicates these by flying to them and calling. The 4–8 white eggs, more elongated than other owls' eggs, are incubated only by the ♀, beginning with the second last laid, for *c.* 28 days. The ♂ feeds her near the nest-hole. Food-remains and pellets are dropped from the hole by the ♀. The young fly when about 4 weeks old. Single-brooded.

Food: Mainly mice, shrews, small birds, lizards, insects.

Remarks: Pygmy owls, often active by day, are recognised by small birds, which "scold" or "mob" them when they appear or sing. Birds living where this owl occurs will begin scolding if a person imitates the song.

Tengmalm's Owl · *Aegolius funereus* (L.) (Illustration precedes p. 246)

Family: Owls (Strigidae)

Description: The upperside is dark brown with white spots. The underside is whitish with dark droplet-like spots. The iris is bright yellow. Juveniles are almost uniformly chocolate-brown with paler bellies and whitish eyebrows and cheek-patches. L: *c.* 10″, Wt: *c.* 4½ oz.

♂♂ show individual variation in the pitch and speed of their song: a swelling "boobooboobooboooboo", of harmonica-like timbre, repeated every 2–3 seconds. When demonstrating the nest-hole the ♂ utters an extended trill. A soft tuning-up note is "muid". When afraid or angry ♂ and ♀ give a snapping "zyuck" or "tyack", also a nasal "kuweck" or "kwehk". Young birds make hoarse, almost toneless "tsit" hunger-calls.

Distribution: The Alps, mountain ranges of central Europe, the Luneburg Heath (N. Germany), Scandinavia, east Europe, the Caucasus, Siberia, North America. It is a resident.

Habitat: On still clear early spring nights unmated ♂♂ sing almost uninterruptedly right through the night. Tree-holes, also nestboxes are used as nest-chambers. 3–7 white eggs are laid on the floor and incubated for 26–28 days by the ♀, fed in the hole by the ♂. Single-brooded.

Food: Predominantly mice, voles and shrews; less often small birds, insects.

Allied species: The long-tailed Hawk Owl (*Surnia ulula*) occurs in north Scandinavia, large stretches of Siberia and northern North America. Its "song" resembles that of Tengmalm's owl.

The nearly eagle owl-sized and largely white Snowy Owl (*Nyctea scandiaca*) breeds in north Scandinavia, Iceland and right around the Arctic region; it occasionally wanders southwards and a pair settled and bred in Shetland in 1967 and have nested there every year since.

BIBLIOGRAPHY

ATKINSON-WILLES, G. L., Wildfowl in Great Britain. London 1963.

AUSTIN, O. L., Birds of the World. London 1961.

BAUER, K. and G. GLUTZ, Handbuch der Vögel Mitteleuropas. Vol 1: Gaviiformes – Phoenicopteriformes. Vols 2 and 3: Anseriformes. Vol 4: Falconiformes Frankfurt 1966–1971.

BROWN, L. and D. AMADON, Eagles, Hawks and Falcons of the World. 2 vols. London 1969.

BROWN, P. E., Birds of Prey. London 1964.

DELACOUR, J., The Waterfowl of the World. 4 vols. London 1954–1964.

DORST, J., The Migration of Birds. London 1962.

FISHER, J., The Shell Bird Book. London 1966.

GLUTZ VON BLOTZHEIM, U., Die Brutvögel der Schweiz. Aarau 1962.

GOODERS, J., Where to Watch Birds. London 1967.

GOODWIN, D., Instructions to Young Ornithologists II – Bird Behaviour. London 1961.

—, Pigeons and Doves of the World. London 1967.

GROSSMAN, M. and J. HAMLET, Birds of Prey of the World. London 1964.

HOLLOM, P. A. D., The Popular Handbook of British Birds (4th edition). London 1968.

LANDSBOROUGH-THOMSON, Sir A., A New Dictionary of Birds. London 1965.

LISTER, M., The Bird Watcher's Reference Book. London 1956.

LOCKLEY, R. M., The Book of Bird Watching. London 1968.

MACLEOD, R. D., Key to the Names of British Birds. London 1954.

MURTON, R. K. and E. N. WRIGHT, The Problems of Birds as Pests (Symposium of the Institute of Biology no. 17). London 1968.

NIETHAMMER, G., Handbuch der Deutschen Vogelkunde. 3 vols. Berlin 1937–1942.

NORTH, M. and E. SIMMS, Witherby's Sound Guide to British Birds. London 1969.

PETERSON, R., G. MOUNTFORT and P. A. D. HOLLOM, A Field Guide to the Birds of Britain and Europe. London 1966.

SOPER, T., The Bird Table Book. London 1965.

STAMP, Sir D., Nature Conservation in Britain. London 1969.

VAURIE, C., The Birds of the Palearctic Fauna, Vol I: Passeriformes. London 1959. Vol II: Non-Passeriformes. London 1965.

VOOUS, K. H., Atlas of European Birds. London 1960.

WITHERBY, H. F., et al., The Handbook of British Birds. 5 vols. London 1938–1941.

ABBREVIATIONS OF AUTHORS' NAMES

Baillon	= Louis A. Baillon 1778–1855
Bechst.	= Johann M. Bechstein 1757–1822
Bodd.	= Pieter Boddaert 1730–1796
Brehm	= Christian Ludwig Brehm 1787–1864
Brème	= Marquis François de Brème
Bruch	= Carl Friedrich Bruch 1789–1857
Brünn.	= Merthen Thrane Brünnich 1737–1827
Frivaldszky	= Imre Frivaldszky 1799–1870
Gmel.	= Johann Friedrich Gmelin 1748–1804
Gunn.	= Johann E. Gunnerus 1718–1773
Hablizl	= Carl Ludwig Hablizl 1752–1821

L., (L.)	= Carl von Linné 1707–1778
Lath.	= John Latham 1740–1837
Leisl.	= Johann Philip Achilles Leisler 1771–1813
Montin	= a Swede, dates unknown
Pontopp.	= Erik Ludwigsen Pontoppidan 1689–1774
Savigny	= Marie Jules César Lelorgne Savigny 1777–1851
Scop.	= Giovanni Antonio Scopoli 1723–1788
Temm.	= Conrad Jacob T. Temminck 1778–1858
Tunst.	= Marmaduke Tunstall 1743–1790

INDEX

Figures in **bold** refer to illustrations

LIST OF PHOTOGRAPHERS

(a. = above, b. = below)

A. Aichhorn, Austria: 173a. – W. A. Bajohr, Germany: 20, 29, 32, 61a., 69a., 80a., 100, 148, 172, 201b., 228a. – W. Bechtle, Germany: 236 – H. Bettmann, Germany: 165a. – U. Böcker, Germany: 16b., 193b. – F. Bretzendorfer, Germany: 28a., 28b. – A. Christiansen, Denmark: 4, 56/57, 64b., 68b., 69b., 73a., 81, 121, 136, 141b., 161b., 164, 169, 177, 181b., 184/185, 196a., 197, 205a., 208b., 209a., 209b., 216/217 – E. Erdmann, Germany: 153, 173b. – H. Fischer, Germany: 152a., 225 – Dr H. Franke, Austria: 228b. – Dr O. v. Frisch, Germany: 41 – Dr G. Haas, Germany: 33b., 221b. – W. Haas, Germany: 92 – G. Hanske, Germany: 160a. – H. Hohn, Germany: 120a. – H. Kacher, Germany: 61b., 64a. – Dr. C. König, Germany: 52/53, 84a., 137a., 244b. – H. Landvogt, Germany: 17, 65a., 76/77, 80b., 132, 156b., 157b., 204 – H. Lasswitz, Germany: 101, 112, 113 – A. Limbrunner, Germany: 140b., 189 – I. and Dr W. Makatsch, Germany: 44/45, 49, 156a. – J. Markham, England: 137b. – S. O. Martin, Germany: 65b., 84b. – K. Oblander, Germany: 212/213 – Tierbilder Okapia, Germany: 229 – H. Olsson, Sweden: 85, 157a., 200a. – C. Panzke, Germany: 37 – G. Quedens, Germany: 60b., 116/117, 180a., 237 – H. Rittinghaus, Germany: 160b., 220 – H. Schünemann, Germany: 224 – R. Schuster, Germany: 48 – K. Schwammberger, Germany: 104, 108, 109a., 109b., 125, 128, 140a., 240, 241, 245 – K.-H. Schwammberger, Germany: 105, 124b. – F. Siedel, Germany: 149 – D. Skruzny, Germany: 176, 181a. – Dr W. Stehle, Germany: 24a., 93, 97a., 97b., 124a., 152b. – H. Steidl, Germany: 141a. – M. Strauss, Germany: 96, 244a. – M. Temme, Germany: 72b., 73b., 145 – A. Thielemann, Germany: 161a. – H. Tomanek, Germany: 232/233 – M. Verbruggen, Belgium: 16a., 21a., 21b., 24b., 25, 40b., 120b., 168, 196b., 201a., 205b., 221a. – K. Weber, Switzerland: 33a., 192b., 193a., 200b. – Dr W. v. Westernhagen, Germany: 60a., 68a., 72a., 180b., 192a. – Dr J.-P. Wittenburg, Germany: 133a., 133b. – W. Zimmermann, Germany: 36 – D. Zingel, Germany: 40a., 88/89, 129, 144a., 144b., 165b., 188, 208a.

Raptors in Flight drawing on p. 14 by Dr C. König